*Philadelphia's Independence Hall—a courtyard
perspective in 1787. Courtesy: National Independence
Historical Park.*

Well Begun

Well Begun

CHRONICLES OF THE EARLY NATIONAL PERIOD

Stephen L. Schechter and Richard B. Bernstein, Editors

New York State Commission on the Bicentennial of the
United States Constitution • Albany, New York

Well Begun: Chronicles of the Early National Period
© New York State Commission on the Bicentennial of the U.S. Constitution
Printed in the United States of America
Published 1989 by the New York State Commission on the Bicentennial of the U.S. Constitution
Distributed with the assistance of the New York State Education Department, Division
of Research and Collections

Library of Congress Cataloguing in Publication Data
Main entry under title:
Well begun: chronicles of the early national period.
1. United States—Politics and government—1789-1797. 2. United States—Capital and
capitol—History—18th century. 3. New York (N.Y.)—Politics and government—To 1898. 4. United
States—Constitutional history.
I. Schechter, Stephen L., 1945- ; Richard B. Bernstein
II. New York State Commission on the Bicentennial of the United States Constitution.
E311.W45 1989 974.7'103—dc19 89-3085
ISBN 0-945660-00-6

Designed by Rich Kraham Design Unit: Eileen Rosenthal

Title page: (Detail) *Washington reviewing the western
army at Fort Cumberland, Maryland. Oil on canvas by
Kemmelmeyer. Courtesy: The Metropolitan Museum of
Art, gift of Edgar William and Bernice Chrysler
Garbisch, 1963.*

To Richard B. Morris ✍ 1904-1989

Whose energy, integrity, and scholarship set a standard for us all.

CONTENTS

FOREWORD

This publication, celebrating the bicentennial anniversary of the establishment of our national government, draws upon the talents of fourteen eminent historians. Their contributions freeze a moment in the history of this country when New York City hosted the inauguration of George Washington and enthusiastically became the first federal capital.

The essays that follow capture the sense of challenge facing those individuals who shaped the institutions which have served us well for two centuries. No one better understood the full implications of this challenge than the individuals who accepted it; and no one better symbolizes that understanding than George Washington as first president of the United States.

What an overwhelming experience it must have been to ''walk on untrodden ground,'' as Washington put it. ''There is scarcely any part of my conduct which may not hereafter be drawn into precedent.'' Younger men, like Thomas Jefferson and Alexander Hamilton, may have wished that Washington navigated that ground more quickly and toward their direction. Later generations can be thankful that Washington was ''slow in operation,'' but, as Jefferson conceded, ''sure in conclusion.''

George Washington had the instinct to govern. At the same time, Washington had an unrelenting commitment to the republican principle of government limited by popular consent and the rule of law, and this remains his greatest contribution to those who must follow in his path. As Washington stated in his First Inaugural Address:

> *The Preservation of the sacred fire of liberty, and the destiny of the Republican model of Government, are justly considered as* deeply, *perhaps as* finally *staked, on the experiment entrusted to the hands of the American people.*

Washington was not alone in understanding and responding to the delicate needs of government in republican society. Vice President John Adams had written a treatise on constitutional government which had guided scores of state constitution makers in their work. Congressman James Madison of Virginia had listened when his constituents demanded the constitutional protection of their civil liberties, championing the movement for the Bill of Rights in the First Federal Congress. Chief Justice John Jay understood the need for the administration from the bench of ''certain & speedy'' justice, as he put it, but he also understood that preservation of justice ultimately depended on a freedom-loving people. In his first address as chief judge of the State of New York, Jay remarked:

> *Every member of the State ought diligently to read and study the constitution of his country, and teach the rising generation to be free. By knowing their rights, they will sooner perceive when they are violated, and be the better prepared to defend and assert them.*

The essays that follow recapture the spirit of these and other Founders as they dedicated themselves to republican government. It is our earnest hope that these essays will, in a small way, remind succeeding generations of the remarkable achievements of this founding generation which were, indeed, ''Well begun.''

Sol Wachtler

EDITORS' INTRODUCTION

More than two thousand years before the inauguration of George Washington in 1789, Plato formulated the criterion upon which all founders are judged and from which the title of this book is drawn—"Well begun is half done." The idea is simple: Countries must be founded on good principles, framed by good constitutions, and formed by good institutions, on the chance that future generations will not always make good public choices.

The history of civilization is filled with stories both real and legendary of men and women who have faced the challenge of founding civil societies capable of meeting the needs of succeeding generations. Nowhere is this more in evidence than in North America, settled nearly two centuries before Washington's inauguration by men and women who founded communities in the wilderness—"as a city on a hill," in the phrase of Governor John Winthrop of Massachusetts Bay—and fought to preserve their devotion to their founding ideas and ideals. These men and women laid the foundation on which George Washington and others of his time would erect the "grand federal edifice" at the Federal Convention of 1787, the ratification controversy of 1787-1788, and the inauguration of 1789.

The events of April 1789, which marked the launching of government under the Constitution, were at the same time a new beginning for the American people and the latest link in a series of foundings and great experiments in government. Thus, we can best understand the Founders of 1789 and their achievements as extensions of the past and as pointers for the future, as participants in an ongoing process of discussion and argument over how to construct the good society and instruments and institutions of government designed to achieve that goal. To that end, the essays in this book explore the founding of 1789, a vital yet largely unappreciated stage in that continuing conversation about human nature, society, government, and politics.

THE WORLD OF THE FOUNDERS

This book is as much a tribute to those who paved the way to 1789 as it is a chronicle of the challenges of that time and those who faced them. The Founders of 1789 had many teachers and many sources of wisdom. They were students of the Enlightenment as well as practical statesmen. As such, they believed that it was within the capacity of the human mind to discover scientifically great principles of government as well as of the natural world. The prologue by Richard B. Bernstein, "The Intellectual World of the Revolutionary Generation," develops this theme, reviewing the intellectual sources, shortcomings, and lasting contributions that the Americans of the revolutionary era made to government and politics.

In "The Constitutional Framework," Richard B. Morris reminds us that the Constitution of the United States, framed two years before the founding of 1789, structured the task of putting it into effect, both empowering and restricting those who launched the national government. Morris focuses on why the delegates to the Federal Convention of 1787 built into the Constitution the doctrine of separation of powers, and how they ensured that those powers were shared and mixed because of the importance they attached to the complementary doctrine of checks and balances.

Morris's essay takes on added importance because many of the Constitution's Framers played major roles in developing the outline of a government they had agreed on in 1787. For example, Alexander Hamilton, an uncompromisingly nationalist Convention delegate from New York, subsequently wrote many pathbreaking essays on national power, public administration, and finance for *The Federalist*, and then carried out and refined his ideas on these subjects as the first secretary of the treasury. James Madison of Virginia, a principal architect of the Constitution and author of most of the *Federalist* essays on Congress, served as a representative from Virginia in that body, where he became the foremost member of the House, a powerful voice for legislative power and responsibility, and the leading spokesman for the need for a bill of rights. William Paterson of New Jersey, who introduced the New Jersey Plan in the Convention, and Oliver Ellsworth of Connecticut, who led the effort to adopt the Great Compromise that saved the Convention, served together in the United States Senate, where they collaborated with fellow Convention delegate and senator, Caleb Strong of Massachusetts, in framing the Judiciary Act of 1789, and later on the United States Supreme Court organized by that statute.

From intellectual world and constitutional framework, we turn to New York City, which as our first capital under the Constitution, was the setting for the founding of 1789. "New Yorkers," writes Kenneth R. Bowling, "who had been busily constructing new docks, repaving streets, and undertaking other civic improvements, determined almost immediately to convert City Hall at Wall and Nassau streets into an elegant building for the First Federal Congress."* However, neither the speedy reconstruction of Federal Hall under the supervision of Pierre L'Enfant nor the hospitality of New Yorkers could keep the federal capital in New York City. In "New York City: The First Federal Capital," Bowling details the battle that New Yorkers, Philadelphians, and other Americans fought over the location of the permanent capital and reconstructs its ideological significance. The resulting Residence Act of July 1790 provided, to the disappointment of both New Yorkers and Philadelphians, that the United States capital would be established on the Potomac River in 1800 and that, in the meantime, Congress would reside in Philadelphia.

In his study of "The First Federal Elections," which rounds out our grouping of essays on the world of the Founders of 1789, Gordon DenBoer reminds us that these elections were "the essential link between the ratification of the Constitution and the First Federal Congress." DenBoer describes how the first representatives, senators, president, and vice president were elected, and why New York State failed to participate in the first Electoral College.

The Work of the Founders

Who were the Founders of 1789 and what were the tasks they faced? The remaining essays collected in this book address these questions.

Congress was the first of the new institutions of national government to commence its work, and the appointed day of its convening (March 4, 1789) was celebrated throughout New York City—although both houses did not secure a quorum until April 6. The first session of the First Federal Congress accomplished the work of a "second constitutional convention." In "Setting Precedent: The First Session of the First Federal Congress," Charlene Bangs Bickford sets out the many accomplishments of that body, including the creation of the first federal executive departments, the organization of the federal court system, and the drafting of the Bill of Rights. Bickford then turns from the task of institution building to one group of congressional institution builders in her case study, "New York's Delegation in the First Federal Congress."

The next three essays chart the inaugural trip, the inauguration, and the administration of George Washington, the first president of the United States. In his essay, "George Washington's Inaugural Trip to New York," John P. Riley chronicles one of the great triumphal processions in our history and, at the same time, takes note of George Washington's mixed feelings about his journey, exemplified by a rare diary entry Washington made on April 16, 1789, the day he left home: "About ten o'clock I bade adieu to Mount Vernon, to private life, and to domestic felicity; and with a mind oppressed with more anxious and painful sensations than I have words to express, set out for New York . . . with the best dispositions to render service to my country in obedience to its call, but with less hope of answering its expectations." Riley's essay then chronicles Washington's two-week journey, during which both he and the American people made the transition from a people in revolution to a nation inventing itself.

The drama of the first presidential inauguration is the subject of Richard B. Bernstein's essay, "The Inauguration of George Washington," which also examines Washington's first Inaugural Address. In his essay "'I Walk on Untrodden Ground:' George Washington as President, 1789-1797," Bernstein outlines the presidential roles established by Washington, including those of head of state, chief executive, policy initiator, consensus builder, treaty maker, and commander in chief. He also describes the extraordinary burdens of the presidency, and the toll they took on Washington.

President Washington was the first and, for several months, virtually the only executive official of the new national government. By the end of 1789, however, Congress had passed and the president had signed into law statutes creating the Department of State (July 27), the Department of War (August 7), the Department of the

Treasury (September 2), the Office of Attorney General (established by the Judiciary Act of 1789 on September 24), and the Office of Postmaster General (commissioned on September 26).

Beginning with a clean slate, the new national government gradually took on public functions in response to the needs and expectations of the time. Among the first public responsibilities assumed by national government in 1789 were the conduct of foreign affairs; collection of customs revenue; collection of tonnage dues; settlement of accounts between the states and the United States; organization and management of the army; government of the Northwest Territory; establishment of lighthouses, beacons, buoys, and public piers; negotiations with Indian tribes; registration and clearance of vessels; conduct of fiscal affairs; safekeeping of acts, records, and the seal of the United States; carrying of mails; conduct of judicial business; prosecution of suits; legal advice to the president and department heads; payment of pensions to disabled veterans; and custody of prisoners.[1]

In ''The Great Departments: The Origin of the Federal Government's Executive Branch,'' Richard Allan Baker describes the beginnings of the executive branch and its first departments and offices. According to Baker, the Treasury Department was the largest and most important federal department. It had a wide range of responsibilities, a detailed congressional mandate, the vital task of raising revenue, and an energetic secretary, Alexander Hamilton, one of two New Yorkers in the first rank of the Founders of 1789. At the end of 1789, Baker reports, the Treasury Department's central office included six chief officers, three principal clerks, twenty-eight clerks, and two messengers. Within a year, that number had nearly doubled. By 1801, the Treasury Department employed more than half of all federal government workers, including a field staff of 1,600 revenue collectors. The Treasury Department was, in many ways, the extended shadow of its first secretary, who Joanne B. Freeman profiles with careful attention to his personality and his policies in her illuminating essay, '''Very busy and not a little anxious': Alexander Hamilton, America's First Secretary of the Treasury.''

Like the executive branch, the federal judiciary had its chief institution (the Supreme Court) established in the Constitution along with constitutional authorization for the creation ''of such inferior Courts as the Congress may from time to time ordain and establish'' (Article III, Section 1). The task of creating the federal court system and deciding how it would relate to existing state court systems fell to the First Federal Congress. In ''The Birth of the Federal Court System,'' David Eisenberg, Christine R. Jordan, Maeva Marcus, and Emily F. Van Tassel discuss the place of the Constitution's Article III in the ratification controversy, the congressional debate over its implementation, and the provisions of the Judiciary Act of September 24, 1789. As the authors note, that act established a working judicial system that "pleased no one completely," but kept its original structure until 1891.

Until the adoption of the Judiciary Act of 1891, which created a separate level of appellate circuit courts, the justices of the United States Supreme Court served both as members of that body and as members of the federal circuit courts. This dual responsibility forced them to "ride circuit"—a difficult and time-consuming responsibility that exhausted and vexed virtually every member of the Supreme Court. In his essay, "John Jay: Federalist and Chief Justice," Herbert Alan Johnson details the achievements on circuit and on the Supreme Court of John Jay of New York, the first chief justice of the United States and the other first-ranking New Yorker among the Founders of 1789. Johnson recounts Jay's resentment of and frustrations with the onerous task of circuit riding over poor highways, the long absences from his family, and the impropriety of subjecting circuit court decisions of colleagues to review by the Supreme Court to which those colleagues also belonged. Johnson also describes Jay's achievement in establishing the rules of practice before the U.S. Supreme Court—a task he tackled "with some degree of assurance," Johnson writes, "because he had been faced with a similar situation when he had become chief justice of New York twleve years earlier." In so doing, Chief Justice Jay, like President Washington, established important institutional traditions, of which perhaps the most important was the Court's refusal to give an advisory opinion to the president.

On September 25, 1789, one day after passing the Judiciary Act, the First Federal Congress proposed its most significant measure, the Bill of Rights, which was sent to the states for ratification as the first amendments to the new Constitution. The lack of a bill of rights had been the single most important and telling objection raised by opponents to the Constitution in 1787-1788. In fact, the Constitution was adopted largely because leading Federalists, including James Madison, agreed to work to add a bill of rights to the Constitution and to take Antifederalists' recommendations into account in that process. Although Madison kept his word, and drew extensively on recommended amendments compiled by Antifederalist delegates to the states' ratifying conventions, emotions continued to run high on the issue, and many Federalist legislators in the First Federal Congress remained unconvinced that a bill of rights was necessary. In "Congress Proposes the Bill of Rights," John P. Kaminski assesses how Congress grappled with this issue and how they finally agreed to resolve it.

The Founders Remembered

Writing in 1814, twenty-five years after George Washington's inauguration and fifteen years after his death, Thomas Jefferson summarized Washington's unique position among the revolutionary generation of Americans—and the Founders of 1789:

> *His was the singular destiny and merit of leading the armies of his country successfully through an arduous war for the establishment of its independence, of conducting its councils through the birth of a government, new in its form and principles, until it settled down into a quiet and orderly train; and of scrupulously obeying the laws through the whole of his career, civil and military, of which the history of the world furnishes no other example.*

Seventy-five years later, the centennial celebration of 1889 of Washington's inauguration and the establishment of the national government was one of the most spectacular historical commemorations in the nation's annals. In the epilogue to this book, ''The Centennial Commemoration of George Washington's Inauguration,'' Richard B. Bernstein chronicles the spectacles of naval flotillas, formal banquets, fireworks, parades, and dedications that marked the centennial observances. He also shows how the Americans of the Gilded Age revealed themselves and their values in the manner of their salute to the Founders of 1789.

Today, as the nation marks the bicentennial of the establishment of our national government, we choose to remember the Founders of 1789 with this book about the extraordinary challenges they faced and their achievements in meeting those challenges. We hope that others will gain a better understanding of how our national government was established, of the challenges and pitfalls contained in the work of founding a government, and of the continuing importance that our national experiment in constitutional government was ''well begun.''

Stephen L. Schechter and Richard B. Bernstein

---

*Completed in early 1789 and immortalized by Peter LaCour's engraving done at the time of Washington's inauguration, the original Federal Hall was later demolished along with all other eighteenth-century public buildings in New York City except Saint Paul's Chapel. The present Federal Hall, located on the site of the original building, was constructed in the nineteenth century, and bears no resemblance to the original building. It is now administered as a national memorial by the National Park Service.

[1]Leonard D. White, *The Federalists: A Study in Administrative History* (New York: Macmillan, 1948), Appendix II, 519. This book is the first in a series of studies by White on the history of American public administration. White's *The Federalist*, which deserves to be returned to print, is the place to begin for those interested in more detail and insights of abiding value on the early years of the new national government.

ACKNOWLEDGMENTS

This publication benefits from the contributions of many individuals who have graciously shared their formidable knowledge of the early years of the Republic. Each author is extended our deepest appreciation for his or her timely and cordial responses to our requests and questions.

We also express our gratitude to the following individuals who made many worthwhile suggestions: Michael Kammen of Cornell University; William Ayres of Fraunces Tavern Museum; Paul Scudiere, New York State Historian; Wendell Tripp of the New York State Historical Association, and James Corsaro of the New York State Library.

The illustrations have been compiled from a number of repositories without whose kind assistance this publication would have been the poorer. We would especially like to thank the Donaldson, Lufkin, and Jenrette Collection of Americana; Indpendence National Historical Park; the Thomas Gilcrease Institute of American History and Art, Tulsa, Oklahoma; The New-York Historical Society; the Bureau of Historic Sites, New York State Office of Parks, Recreation and Historic Preservation; the National Archives; the New York Public Library; The Museum of Fine Arts, Boston; The Henry Francis duPont Winterthur Museum; the Museum of the City of New York; the Museum of American Folk Art; Life Picture Service; the Johns Hopkins University Press; the New York City Commission on the Bicentennial of the Constitution; the National Portrait Gallery of the Smithsonian Institution; the Mount Vernon Ladies' Association of the Union; the New York State Museum, Division of Research and Collections; Fraunces Tavern Museum; the Society for the Preservation of New England Antiquities; the Supreme Court Historical Society; the Library of Congress, and Yale University Library (Franklin Papers); Ene Sirvet, associate editor of *The Papers of John Jay*, Columbia University; Kym S. Rice; and Peter S. Kohlmann, executive director of the New York City Commission on the Bicentennial of the Constitution.

A special word of thanks goes to Shirley Rice, publications director of the New York State Bicentennial Commission. She managed this complex project, copy edited its pages, and kept it on schedule without jeopardizing other publication needs of the commission.

◆　◆　◆

On March 3, 1989, as the last essays in this book were going to press, Professor Richard B. Morris died in New York City at the age of eighty-four. For more than six decades, Professor Morris was a preeminent historian of the United States. His many books and articles record his pathbreaking contributions to legal, social, labor, economic, diplomatic, intellectual, political, and constitutional history. His devotion to teaching, to recovering the record of the past (exemplified by *The Papers of John Jay*), and to bringing history to a general audience, most recently as co-chair of Project '87, are models for his colleagues. We are honored that this book includes an essay by Professor Morris, and we record in the dedication our indebtedness to him.

PROLOGUE

The Intellectual World of the Revolutionary Generation

by Richard B. Bernstein

As the people of the United States prepared to launch their new form of government in 1789, virtually every nation in the western world was feeling the winds of change unleashed by the American Revolution. Ideas and ideals of liberty and self-government were popular as never before; the dream of codifying laws of human nature, society, politics, and government—a dream shared by all who lived in the Age of Enlightenment—seemed within human grasp. The American republic may have been on the periphery of western civilization as a matter of geography and of cultural snobbishness, but the Americans believed themselves destined to point the way to a new era of government, and they had reason to believe it.[1]

To the aristocratic philosophers of Europe, the United States was an odd proving ground for advances in the art of government.[2] Indeed, for most of their history as an independent nation the Americans apparently could not decide whether they were a nation or not.[3] The United States consisted of thirteen states strung together along the Atlantic coast; under the 1783 Treaty of Paris the Americans claimed land extending to the Mississippi River. This vast territory was larger than any European nation except Russia, and most of the American states were as large as world powers like Britain or France. And yet the Americans could only boast a population of 3,600,00; their largest city, Philadelphia, numbered about 40,000. Nine out of every ten citizens made their living off the land in whole or in part; almost no one traveled more than five miles from his or her birthplace in a lifetime. The Americans worked hard for their livelihood, yet managed to maintain a standard of living as high as any in the Atlantic civilization.[4]

In virtually all of the thirteen states, part of this standard of living was built on the backs of black slaves. More than 600,000 men, women, and children were held in bondage in this period—a mute but ever-present contradiction of the Americans' revolutionary ideology of liberty, equality, and natural rights. At the height of the Revolution, the British literary giant Samuel Johnson demanded to know why it was that the loudest ''yelps for liberty'' came from ''the drivers of negroes.'' In response to the growling hostility to chattel slavery, such Americans as Benjamin Franklin, John Jay, and Alexander Hamilton organized anti-slavery and manumission societies and African Free Schools; and some states, chiefly in New England, had taken steps to abolish the institution. Nonetheless, the Constitution ratified in 1788 recognized slavery's existence (albeit without explicitly using the word), building it into the document's formulas for representation and taxation.[5]

SOURCES OF POLITICAL CREATIVITY
American politicians of the revolutionary period were both intellectuals and practical statesmen. They drew on the accumulated wisdom of western civilizations; they also benefitted from nearly two centuries of experience of self-government in the New World. Thus, to a greater extent than any subsequent generation of American politicians, the leaders of the Revolutionary generation approached the ideal of the ''philosopher kings'' postulated by Plato. What were the sources of their political wisdom and creativity?[6]

First, the new nation began its existence among the ruins of the British Empire and derived from that ex-

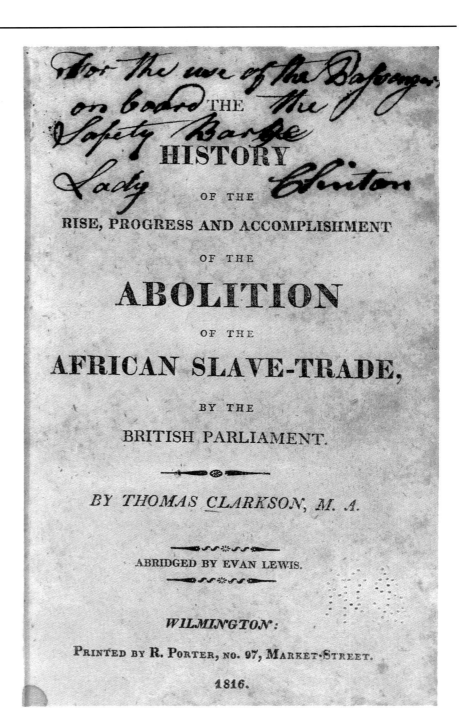

perience important lessons about the possibilities and limitations of constitutional government. The Americans' dispute with the mother country was a constitutional dispute: American politicians and British officials held two distinct and conflicting conceptions of the English constitution and its applicability to British North America. Recent scholarship had delineated the clash of the two constitutions and restored legitimacy to the Americans' constitutional arguments. The Americans' conception of the English constitution as a guard against any form of arbitrary power was rooted in the English Civil War of the 1640s; the English conception of their constitution as one enshrining parliamentary supremacy was a product of the experience of the eighteenth century. The dispute could not be resolved for there was no final judicial or other authority to whom both sides could submit the controversy with confidence in the justice of the ultimate outcome. Although the Americans won their independence in the war that followed the breakdown of constitutional argument, problems of balancing the need for central authority against the claims of state and local government and individual liberty continued to plague the United States.[7]

The leading politicians of the new nation drew on other sources of ideas and experience as well. In addition to the English constitution, they were learned in the common law, and valued its protections of individual liberty.[8] Well versed in classical and Renaissance literature, and in the history of Greek, Roman, and Italian republics, they also possessed a profound understanding of the strengths and weaknesses of republican government.[9] Products of a civilization and culture that inculcated the values of the Judeo-Christian tradi-

tion, they absorbed and applied the important ideal of the covenant to the task of constructing instruments and institutions of government.[10] Steeped in the experience of government of their respective colonies and states, they also knew first-hand (and many had taken part in) the process of framing new constitutions of government in the 1770s and 1780s for their states. In restoring legitimate government to the states, they also produced important and far-reaching innovations in government, among them the written declaration of rights and the independently elected chief executive.[11] Above all else, they were children of the Age of Enlightenment, and as such believed in the power of reason in human affairs. Just as Isaac Newton had identified and elucidated the laws of physics, they believed, it was possible to identify and elucidate laws of human behavior, including general and immutable principles of government. To preserve liberty was their great aim; yet they believed that liberty could be preserved only through a thorough study and understanding of human nature by devising forms of government based on that source of wisdom. Many of the younger generation of American statesmen especially were driven by this bold and generous ambition to be the Newton of government—Alexander Hamilton, James Madison, James Wilson, and Charles Pinckney among them.[12] Even those statesmen who did not take part directly in the framing of the Constitution—John Adams, Thomas Jefferson, and John Jay—exerted an indirect influence through framing or proposing constitutions of government for their individual states.[13]

The Americans had experienced a remarkable age of experiments in government. First, as noted above, they had had to frame new structures of government for the states to replace the

colonial charters toppled by the Revolution. Second, they had had to frame two charters of government for the United States—the Articles of Confederation, and then the United States Constitution. In turn, the making of the Constitution had two distinct stages: its framing in Philadelphia at the Federal Convention of 1787 and its ratification by the people of the several states in 1787 and 1788. Finally, they had to make this new, untried instrument of government work. That task is the subject of this book.

Neither the framing nor the adoption of the Constitution was foreordained, nor was the success of the new form of government guaranteed. As would be proved in blood and slaughter seventy-five years later, the revolutionary generation had not solved perhaps the most agonizing quandary of American politics: the relationship between slavery and federalism.[14] Nonetheless, as those who sought to defend the Union and the Constitution in the 1860s maintained, it took the creation and development of a federal government under the Constitution of 1787 to produce a power strong enough to deal the death's blow to the institution of chattel slavery.[15] As illustrated by the experience of the Civil War and Reconstruction, the history of the United States under the Constitution is a story of how the American people have experimented with the power of government to solve national problems without endangering individual liberty.[16] This experiment was made possible in the first place by the labors of the revolutionary generation.

The process of forging a government for ourselves and our posterity is of necessity an open-ended one. As Bill Moyers had pointed out, ''If these men got a republic started through deliberation, then certainly we can keep it going by imagining ourselves their heirs of civil discourse.''[17] The men whose labors are chronicled in these pages left us a constitutional legacy including the obligation to carry on their work. Our task is that articulated by President Lyndon B. Johnson twenty-five years ago: ''Let us continue.''

[1]See generally R.R. Palmer, *The Age of the Democratic Revolution,* 2 vols. (Princeton: Princeton University Press, 1959, 1964); Henry Steele Commager, *The Empire of Reason* (1977; New York: Oxford University Press, 1981).

[2]On the *philosophes*, and on the contrast between the European and American Enlightenments, see generally Commager, *Empire of Reason*; also the essays collected in Henry Steele Commager, *Jefferson, Nationalism, and the Enlightenment* (New York: Brazilier, 1975).

[3]This is a major theme of Richard B. Bernstein with Kym S. Rice, *Are We to Be a Nation? The Making of the Constitution* (Cambridge, Mass.: Harvard University Press, 1987).

[4]See generally Bernstein with Rice, *Are We to Be a Nation?*, 1-10 and sources cited.

[5]See the works cited in note 11 below.

[6]See Commager, *Empire of Reason, passim*; Bernstein with Rice, *Are We to Be a Nation?*, chap. 5; Forrest McDonald, *Novus Ordo Seclorum: The Intellectual Origins of the Constitution* (Lawrence: University Press of Kansas, 1985). See also Henry Steele Commager, ''Leadership in Eighteenth-Century America and Today,'' in *Freedom and Order* (New York: Brazilier, 1988).

[7]The leading student of this subject is Professor John Phillip Reid of New York University Law School. His works on this subject include *In a Defiant Stance* (State College, Pa.: Pennsylvania State University Press, 1977); *In a Rebellious Spirit* (State College, Pa.: Penn State University Press, 1979); *In Defiance of the Law* (Chapel Hill, N.C.: University of North Carolina Press, 1981); *The Briefs of*

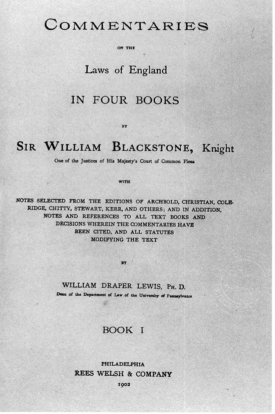

COMMENTARIES

ON THE

Laws of England

IN FOUR BOOKS

BY

SIR WILLIAM BLACKSTONE, Knight

One of the Justices of His Majesty's Court of Common Pleas

WITH

NOTES SELECTED FROM THE EDITIONS OF ARCHBOLD, CHRISTIAN, COLERIDGE, CHITTY, STEWART, KERR, AND OTHERS; AND IN ADDITION, NOTES AND REFERENCES TO ALL TEXT BOOKS AND DECISIONS WHEREIN THE COMMENTARIES HAVE BEEN CITED, AND ALL STATUTES MODIFYING THE TEXT

BY

WILLIAM DRAPER LEWIS, Ph. D.

Dean of the Department of Law of the University of Pennsylvania

BOOK I

PHILADELPHIA
REES WELSH & COMPANY
1902

the American Revolution (New York: New York University Press, 1981); Constitutional History of the American Revolution, vol. 1: The Authority of Rights (Madison; University of Wisconsin Press, 1986), and vol. 2: The Authority to Tax (Madison: University of Wisconsin Press, 1987) (the third and final volume, ''The Authority to Legislate,'' is in progress); and The Concept of Liberty in the Era of the American Revolution (Chicago: University of Chicago Press, 1988). (Another monograph, The Concept of Representation in the Era of the American Revolution, will be published in late 1989 by the University of Chicago Press). See also Reid's challenging essay, ''The Irrelevance of the Declaration,'' pp. 16-85 in Hendrik Hartog, ed., Law in the American Revolution and the Revolution in the Law (New York: New York University Press, 1981). On the persistent problems plaguing both the British and the American constitutional systems, see Jack P. Greene, Peripheries and Center (Athens: University of Georgia Press, 1986).

[8]See, e.g., Hartog, ed.; Law in the American Revolution and the Revolution in the Law; on the experience of a specific state; William E. Nelson, Americanization of the Common Law: The Impact of Legal Change on Massachusetts, 1760-1830 (Cambridge, Mass.: Harvard University Press, 1975); on Blackstone and his influence, Daniel J. Boorstin, The Mysterious Science of the Law (1941; Boston: Beacon Press, 1958).

[9]Meyer Reinhold, Classica Americana (Detroit: Wayne State University Press, 1984); J.G.A. Pocock, The Machiavellian Moment (Princeton: Princeton University Press, 1975); J.G.A. Pocock, Virtue, Commerce, and History (Cambridge: Cambridge University Press, 1985).

[10]See, e.g., Donald S. Lutz, The Origins of American Constitutionalism (Baton Rouge: Louisiana State University Press, 1988); Daniel J. Elazar, The American Constitutional Tradition (Lincoln: University of Nebraska Press, 1988).

[11]See, e.g., Willi Paul Adams, The First American Constitutions (Chapel Hill: University of North Carolina Press, 1980); Donald S. Lutz, Popular Consent and Popular Control: Whig Political Theory in the First State Constitutions (Baton Rouge: Louisiana State University Press, 1980); Bernstein with Rice, Are We to Be a Nation?, chap. 3.

[12]Bernstein with Rice, Are We to Be a Nation?, 158. See generally Douglass Adair, Fame and the Founding Fathers, ed. Trevor Colburn (New York: Norton, 1974) and Richard R. Beeman, Stephen Botein, and Edward C. Carter, II, eds., Beyond Confederation (Chapel Hill: University of North Carolina Press, 1987). On Hamilton, see Gerald Stourzh, Alexander Hamilton and the Idea of Republican Government (Stanford: Stanford University Press, 1970), and the essay by Joanne B. Freeman in this volume. On Madison, see Irving Brant, James Madison (6 vols.; Indianapolis: Bobbs-Merrill, 1911-1961), esp. vols. 2 and 3, and Robert A. Rutland, James Madison: The Founding Father (New York: Macmillan, 1987). Garry Wills is preparing a study of James Wilson.

[13]Bernstein with Rice, Are We to Be a Nation?, chap. 3.

[14]See generally Donald L. Robinson, Slavery and the Structure of American Politics, 1765-1820 (New York: Harcourt Brace Jovanovich, 1971); Paul Finkelman, An Imperfect Union: Slavery, Federalism, and Comity (Chapel Hill: University of North Carolina Press, 1981); Winthrop D. Jordan, White over Black: American Attitudes Towards Slavery and the Negro, 1558-1812 (Chapel Hill: University of North Carolina Press, 1968).

[15]This point is derived from the 1987 annual address at the Convention of the American Society for Legal History by Professor Don E. Fehrenbacker, based on Professor Fehrenbacker's book-length work in progress on the same topic.

[16]On the constitutional consequences of the Civil War and Reconstruction, see, e.g.: J.G. Randall, Constitutional Problems Under Lincoln (1926; rev. ed., Urbana, Ill.: University of Illinois Press, 1951); Harold M. Hyman, A More Perfect Union: The Impact of the Civil War and Reconstruction on the Constitution (New York: Alfred A. Knopf, 1971); Harold M. Hyman and William M. Wiecek, Equal Justice Under Law: Constitutional Development, 1835-1875 (New York: Harper & Row, 1982); Robert J. Kaczorowski, The Politics of Judicial Interpretation (Dobbs Ferry, New York: Oceana Publications, 1985); James M. McPherson, Battle Cry of Freedom: The Civil War Era (New York: Oxford University Press, 1988); and William E. Nelson, The Fourteenth Amendment: From Political Principle to Judicial Doctrine (Cambridge, Mass.: Harvard University Press, 1988).

[17]Bill Moyers, ''Introduction,'' in Bill Moyers, Moyers: Report from Philadelphia (New York: Ballantine, 1987).

Blackstone and title page of his Commentaries.

Well Begun

CHRONICLES OF THE EARLY NATIONAL PERIOD

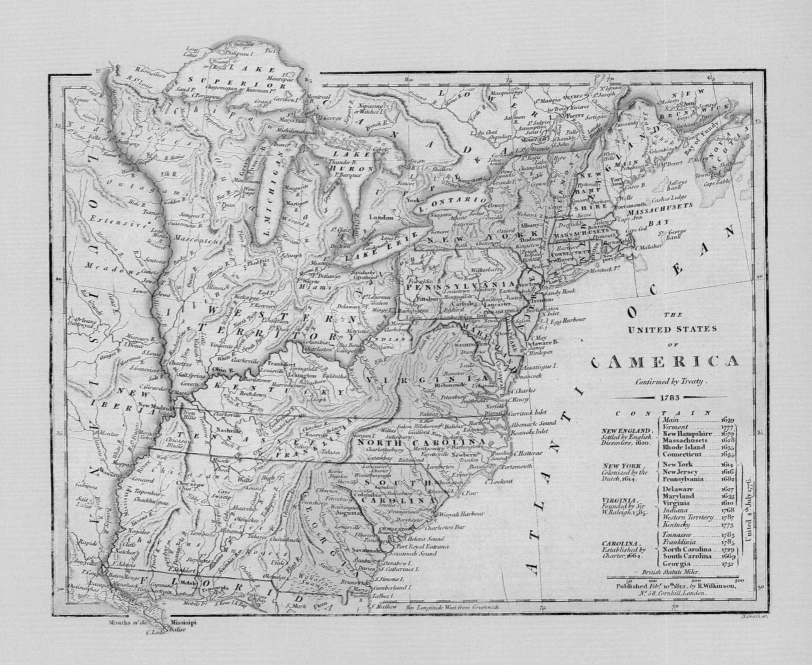

THE
UNITED STATES
OF
CAMERICA
Confirmed by Treaty.
1783

CONTAIN

NEW ENGLAND, Settled by English Dissenters, 1620.	Main	1639
	Vermont	1777
	New Hampshire	1679
	Massachusets	1628
	Rhode Island	1635
	Connecticut	1635
NEW YORK, Colonized by the Dutch, 1614.	New York	1614
	New Jersey	1616
	Pennsylvania	1682
VIRGINIA, Founded by Sir W. Raleigh, 1585.	Delaware	1627
	Maryland	1633
	Virginia	1610
	Indiana	1768
	Western Territory	1787
	Kentucky	1773
CAROLINA, Established by Charter, 1664.	Tennessee	1783
	Franklinia	1785
	North Carolina	1729
	South Carolina	1669
	Georgia	1732

British Statute Miles.

50   100   200   300

Published Feb.ʳ 10.ᵗʰ 1812, by R.Wilkinson,
Nᵒ. 58. Cornhill, London.

United 4ᵗʰ July 1776.

ATLANTIC OCEAN

Mouths of the Missisipi

Longitude West from Greenwich.

The Constitutional Framework

by Richard B. Morris

The inauguration of President George Washington on April 30, 1789 heralded the launching of the new federal Constitution, ratified only the year before. The delegates assembled in Philadelphia at the Constitutional Convention of 1787 had invented a constitution without precedent and at critical points significantly diverging from both the old Articles of Confederation and the British example. The most original, and most characteristic, feature of the Constitution was its incorporation of two seemingly incompatible doctrines: separation of powers and checks and balances.

Implicit in every plan proposed at the Constitutional Convention of 1787 is the idea of separation of powers, but nowhere in the Constitution itself do we find that doctrine either mentioned or spelled out. Although the doctrine roots in the political discourse of English writers of the Cromwellian period such as Clement Walker and Marchamont Nedham, the eighteenth-century French jurist and philosopher Montesquieu provided the authoritative source of the doctrine, and the one most relied on by most American lawmakers. To the extent that he did not insist on an absolute separation of powers, but recognized the necessity of a blending or overlapping of functions (the idea of balanced government), Montesquieu articulated the conviction of American revolutionary and constitutional lawmakers that separation of functions and powers among institutions was necessary to preserve liberty. So, for example, the First Continental Congress had affirmed in its 1774 "Letter to the inhabitants of the Province of Quebec," directly quoting from the "immortal Montesquieu."

From the perspective of separation of

The United States in 1783.

4 powers and checks and balances, the Continental Congress was an anomaly among the Americans' experiments in government. Unlike the state constitutions, many of which reaffirmed ideas of separation of powers and checks and balances, the Continental Congress violated these principles in its own structure, combining executive, legislative, and limited judicial functions. This feature of the Articles of Confederation attracted much criticism.

Of all the Founding Fathers, John Jay of New York, the Confederation's Secretary for Foreign Affairs, had by the eve of the Constitutional Convention emerged as the nationalist who was most consistent in recognizing the need for a system incorporating separation of powers and checks and balances. Those doctrines provide a constant theme in his correspondence. ''I have long thought,'' he wrote Thomas Jefferson in 1786, ''and become daily more convinced, that the construction of our federal government is fundamentally wrong. To vest legislative, judicial, and even executive powers in one and the same body of men, and that, too, in a body daily changing its members, can never be wise. In my opinion, those three great departments of sovereignty should be forever separated, and so distributed as to serve as checks on each other.'' Again, in January 1787, when George Washington solicited Jay's advice in preparation for attending the Convention, Jay was explicit: ''Let Congress legislate. Let others execute. Let others judge.'' Although Jay was not selected to be a Convention delegate, his views were shared by two

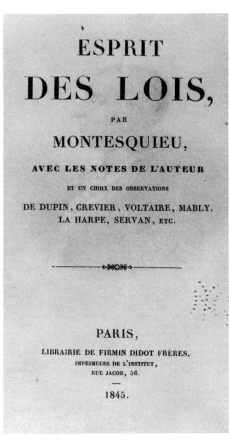

ESPRIT
DES LOIS,
PAR
MONTESQUIEU,
AVEC LES NOTES DE L'AUTEUR
ET UN CHOIX DES OBSERVATIONS
DE DUPIN, CREVIER, VOLTAIRE, MABLY,
LA HARPE, SERVAN, ETC.

PARIS,
LIBRAIRIE DE FIRMIN DIDOT FRÈRES,
IMPRIMEURS DE L'INSTITUT,
RUE JACOB, 56.

1845.

arch-nationalists who were Convention delegates, Alexander Hamilton of New York and James Madison of Virginia. Ideas of separation of powers and checks and balances also formed part and parcel of the intellectual baggage of most of the other delegates.

With this shared doctrinal background among the delegates, it should have come as no surprise that the initial plan of government proposed by Edmund Randolph of Virginia (and inspired by his fellow Virginian, Madison) provided for separation of powers. The cornerstone of the constitutional system as finally adopted embraced separate legislative, executive, and judicial branches, as outlined in Articles I, II, and III of the Constitution. That the proposed new charter also incorporated a system of checks and balances was not seen to be inconsistent with the idea of separation of powers. Madison, for example, did not conceive of separation as a rigorous absolute, and argued that some "deviation" from the principle "must be admitted." Both in his essays in *The Federalist* and in his speeches to the 1788 Virginia ratifying convention, Madison later defended this apparent "deviation" by arguing that the separate branches must be so blended as to give to each a constitutional check upon the other.

In Article I of the Constitution, which created the Congress of the United States, the Convention confined that body to enumerated powers, while also including a list of prohibitions upon the states. Both here and with regard to the other two branches, the delegates did

Far left: *Montesquieu and title page of* The Spirit of the Laws.
Left: *George Washington's Rising Sun chair used during the Constitutional Convention at Independence Hall. When the Constitution was finally signed, Benjamin Franklin remarked, "Now I have the happiness to know that it is a rising, not a setting, sun." Courtesy: Independence National Historical Park.*

6 not follow the recommendation of their colleague John Dickinson of Delaware that the three branches of government ought to be as independent as possible. Again, they sought to restrain these new branches of government through recourse to the doctrine of checks and balances.

Consider the executive branch. Issues of separation of powers and checks and balances were clearly central to the furious debate provoked by the issue of the executive's powers, among them the power to veto laws passed by Congress. The Virginia Plan introduced by Randolph had called for entrusting such power to a council of revision comprising the president and members of the national judiciary—an idea drawn from the New York constitution of 1777. By a narrow margin, the proposed council of revision was rejected in favor of a compromise proposal conferring a qualified rather than an absolute veto power on the president, whose veto could overridden by a two-thirds vote of Congress. In other respects, the president's powers were curtailed. He was given power, for example, to make treaties "by and with the advice and consent of the Senate," but only with the concurrence of two-thirds of the senators present.

We may cite a number of other key instances where the delegates found it expedient to violate strict separation of powers in the name of checks and balances. Thus, Article II, Sec. 4 renders "the President, Vice President and all civil officers of the United States...removable from office by impeachment for, and conviction of Treason, Bribery or other high Crimes and Misdemeanors." The Constitution vests the power of impeachment in the House, and assigns the power to try impeachments to the Senate. Ordinarily, the vice president presides over impeachment trials, carrying out his sole

Secretary of the Confederation Congress Charles Thomson recorded New Hampshire's ratification on July 2, 1788, putting the Constitution into effect. Courtesy: National Archives.
Right: "Scene of the Signing of the U.S. Constitution," by Howard Chandler Christy. Courtesy: U.S. Capitol Collection, Architect of the Capitol.

8 constitutional responsibility as President of the Senate. However, in the extraordinary instance of impeachment of the president, the chief justice shall preside—an extraordinary, if necessary, example of mixed powers.

The war powers provide another example of a mixture of executive and legislative powers—again, a compromise. The power to make war raised significant issues and required the delegates to consider matters of definition and limits with great care. A prudent James Madison, seconded by Elbridge Gerry of Massachusetts, moved to empower Congress to "declare" rather than "make" war, "leaving to the Executive the power to repel sudden attacks." George Mason of Virginia, who declared that the executive was "not safely to be trusted" with the war power, was for "clogging rather than facilitating war, but for facilitating peace." Gerry agreed, declaring in response to a South Carolinian motion to augment executive power in this field that he "never expected to hear in a republic a motion to empower the executive alone to declare war." The motion to amend the powers of Congress over war by inserting "declare" in place of "make" carried by seven states to two.

As finally adopted, the Constitution takes an ambivalent stand on the war powers. Article I, Sec. 8 vests in Congress the power to declare war and to raise and support armies, while limiting appropriations to their use to a maximum of two years. Article II, Sec. 2 describes the president as commander in chief. From this apparent division of powers one might infer that the Convention intended to distinguish between declaring war and supporting it, on the one hand, and conducting its operations on the other. This area of constitutional law has been the source of vigorous controversy for two hundred years.

Although the state judiciary systems were offshoots of the colonial, and they in turn were modeled upon the British, the federal judicial branch as shaped by the Constitution in Article III and by the Judiciary Act of 1789 was a distinct departure from the British system. The Framers treated the role of the federal judiciary with a remarkable economy of words, but sought to guarantee to the judiciary a great deal of independence. True, the federal judiciary was to be appointed by the president by and with the advice and consent of the Senate—a power which gives him exceptional influence over the political direction of the federal courts. At the same time, the judges were to hold office during good behavior (a critical issue in pre-Revolutionary days, when colonial judges, appointed by royal governors, could continue in office indefinitely), and their compensation could not be diminished "during their continuance in office" (Article III, Sec. 1). The grant of federal judicial power in Article III is silent on the ever-controversial question of judicial review, leaving room for those on both sides of the question whether judicial exercise of the power to declare federal or state laws unconstitutional raises courts to the level of a "super-legislature" impairing the authority of the legislative branch.

In sum, all the leading delegates at the Constitutional Convention favored creating a national government with energy and power to act to fulfill the magnificent objectives so eloquently stated in the Preamble. At the same time, they deemed the doctrines of separation of powers and checks and balances essential to the preservation of liberty. The delegates did not feel that they had crafted a perfect constitution but were hopeful that they had made a good beginning and that the amendment process delineated in Article V provided a means to correct defects in the performance of the federal government. The inauguration of George Washington, a key moment in the process of breathing life into the constitutional framework drafted in 1787 and adopted in 1788, presaged an era of great constitution building.

New York City:

THE FIRST FEDERAL CAPITAL

by Kenneth R. Bowling

New York City received a splendid Christmas present from the United States government in 1784. On December 23, Congress adopted an ordinance which located the federal capital on the banks of the Delaware River near Trenton, New Jersey, and agreed to meet in New York until completion of the new town. The decision to remain at New York until completion of the new capital reflected a desire to stabilize and revitalize the federal government. Congress had sat at Philadelphia from 1774 to 1783, except when the British army twice forced it to flee. Then, between June 1783 and December 1784, it met in three small towns: Princeton, New Jersey; Annapolis, Maryland; and Trenton, New Jersey. New York City's tenure as the seat of the federal government lasted much longer than congressmen expected because southerners, who disliked the location of the federal town near Trenton, struck out the budget appropriation for it. Consequently, the Congress was bound to remain at New York.

The Confederation Congress convened there in January 1785. Ecstatic New Yorkers welcomed Congress with addresses and a thirteen-gun salute from the Battery. A newspaper editorial declared the event to be of the first magnitude to the city and that it would give New York a great name among nations. The city and it 20,000 residents had not yet recovered from a seven-year occupation by the British army, two devastating fires, and the loss of half of its population and commerce. The arrival of Congress promised revitalization, and New Yorkers welcomed its members accordingly, building a new social life around them.

Delegates found ample accommoda-

This scene of the Tontine Coffee House captures the vitality of Manhattan in the late eighteenth century. Courtesy: The New-York Historical Society.

12 tions; the city provided Congress part of City Hall, and Congress rented space at Fraunces Tavern for the departments of foreign affairs and war. Congressmen described New Yorkers as the most hospitable people. Even Philadelphia partisans admitted to the city's advantages. Sumptuous dinners, crowds of invitations, and a frenzy of visits kept the members entertained during the early weeks of 1785. By the end of the year, elegant private parties, fortnightly concerts, and theater three nights a week provided entertainment. So many members married New York women that one wit dubbed the place, "Calypso's Island." Accustomed to criticizing Philadelphia and the towns in which Congress had previously resided, congressmen embraced New York and complained only about the higher cost of living.

The years that Congress spent at New York witnessed the hoped-for revitalization of the federal government. The welcoming address offered by New York City lavished praise on Congress and called for an augmentation of its powers. The conflicts with the host local and state governments experienced at Philadelphia did not arise at New York. Congress decided to reunite the executive and legislative functions of the federal government and ordered all remaining executive officeholders to New York. Those who argued that they could serve better at Philadelphia were asked to resign. The land ordinances of 1785 and 1787 stand out among the many legislative accomplishments of the Confederation Congress during its tenure at New York.

Nevertheless, southerners disliked residing so far from the center of the Union, and beginning in 1787, they joined Pennsylvanians in attempting to bypass the ordinance of 1784 and return to Philadelphia. They almost succeeded

Map of New York City and the surrounding area ca. 1789. Courtesy: The Johns Hopkins University Press. Right: A view of Broad and Wall streets, New York City, including Federal Hall, ca. 1797. Courtesy: New York Public Library Prints Division, Stokes Collection.

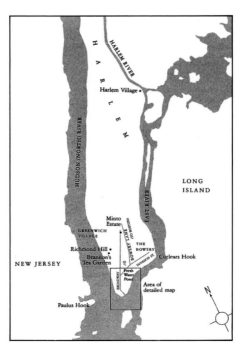

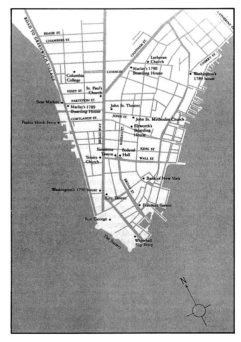

in April 1787, when they argued that Congress should be in Philadelphia to keep an eye on the Constitutional Convention, scheduled to meet in mid-May. The Constitution proposed by that body in September authorized the establishment of a federal district, thus nullifying the 1784 ordinance which had brought Congress to New York. Attempts at the Convention to forbid Congress from including any state capital or large commercial city within the district failed in part because of arguments that such a restriction would create enemies for the Constitution at New York and Philadelphia, two state capitals that desired to become the federal capital.

On July 2, 1788, Congress learned that the necessary nine states had ratified the Constitution and began the process for convening the new federal government. Its task was to set a time and place for the First Federal Congress to assemble and a time for the presidential electors to be chosen and to vote. Debate on the enabling resolution was postponed in hopes that the New York ratifying convention at Poughkeepsie would complete its proceedings in the meantime. The postponement had the effect of a bribe: ratify the Constitution and Congress would likely remain at New York; defeat it, and Congress would have no choice but to leave. On July 26, New York ratified the Constitution, for this and other reasons.

14 Congress took up the postponed resolution immediately. Members knew a major sectional fight was at hand over the question of where the new Congress should convene, but none expected to spend six difficult weeks reaching a decision. One complained that as many cities sought the capital as had contended for the Olympic games in the ancient world. Indeed, as the weeks passed, motions failed for meeting at Annapolis and Baltimore, Maryland; Wilmington, Delaware; Lancaster, Pennsylvania; and Princeton, New Jersey. New York and Philadelphia, however, remained the serious contenders.

While the debate raged, Philadelphians filled their newspapers with attacks on New York: They asserted that the city was not centrally located in the Confederation, its public buildings inadequate and badly situated, and its harbor open to enemy navies. The New York press extolled New York, but also shot back: "Our brethren of the type in Philadelphia seem to be laboring very hard to persuade Congress that *their* city is the only place in the United States fit for the seat of government;" reported the *Independent Journal* on September 6, "indeed they have magnified and praised this *metropolis of America* to such an excess, that it appears the honor will be conferred on Congress (by permitting them to reside there) instead of Congress conferring it upon them."

By late August 1788, Federalists throughout the United States began to worry that implementation of the Constitution was threatened by the bitter debate over the site. Finally, the Philadelphians gave up. "Let the place of meeting be New York" or even "the

Cong.s Embark'd on board the Ship Constitution of America bound to Conogocheque by way of Philadelphia.

banks of the Potomac, Ohio, or Mississippi, let it be anywhere; but for Heaven's sake…let the government be put in motion," declared the *Pennsylvania Mercury* on September 9. Three days later, a member introduced a new ordinance, the seventh to be considered. As a compromise, it avoided naming New York City. The Delaware delegation stormed home in anger just as Marylanders had done a few days earlier. On September 13, Congress adopted an ordinance calling the First Federal Congress to assemble on March 4, 1789, at "the present seat of Congress." New Yorkers lavished praise on Congressman Alexander Hamilton who had led the fight to keep Congress at New York. The choice, as Congressman James Madison, a Philadelphia supporter, informed George Washington, was staying at New York or strangling the new government at birth.

New Yorkers, who had been busily constructing new docks, repaving streets, and undertaking other civic improvements, determined almost immediately to convert City Hall at Wall and Nassau streets into an elegant building for the First Federal Congress. Pierre L'Enfant supervised the conversion of the eighty-five year-old building which had housed the John Peter Zenger freedom of the press trial and the Stamp Act Congress as well as the Confederation Congress. The speed with which the reconstruction took place stunned observers, and Federal Hall, the building's new name, quickly became a symbol for the new government throughout the United States. Its other political implication did not go unnoticed. One Pennsylvania representative, while admitting its elegance,

termed Federal Hall a "trap," constructed to keep Congress at New York. He hoped, however, to escape.

Philadelphians had been active all winter in a campaign to defame New York and convince Americans that the refusal of Congress to leave the city threatened the survival of the Union. They planned to introduce a motion as soon as the First Federal Congress convened that it adjourn immediately to Philadelphia. Madison and the southerners refused to support the effort because it promised to immerse the First Congress into a morass of political wheeling and dealing.

Despite a thirteen-gun salute to the old government on March 3, 1789, and an eleven-gun salute the next morning for the states that had ratified the Constitution, a quorum was not reached until April 6, when Congress convened. The embittered Pennsylvanians complained about the narrow, twisting streets and the cramped environment about Federal Hall. The stench and pollution that some members noted could be avoided by living in the country at Greenwich Village, a mile to the north. For the most part, however, congressmen found the capital a pleasing place to live.

In order to persuade Philadelphia's supporters not to make a motion to leave New York, Madison and others agreed that the question could be considered at the end of the session. Consequently, in September, the Senate passed a bill locating the permanent capital in Pennsylvania, with Congress remaining temporarily at New York. With the help of influential New Yorkers, Madison had the bill proposed to the second session of the First Federal Congress where it was killed.

To induce Congress to remain, New York began construction of a handsome presidential mansion on the Battery.

Nevertheless, in July of 1790, after weeks of politicking and legislative stalemate, Congress adopted, and George Washington signed, the Residence Act. It provided that the United States capital would be established on the Potomac River in 1800 and that, in the meantime, Congress would reside at Philadelphia.

New Yorkers were deeply hurt by the decision, and they expressed anger in the press and in political cartoons. They accused Congress of ingratitude and suggested that the city deserved federal aid as compensation for the relocation. They condemned those Antifederalists whom they believed had voted to ratify the Constitution in 1788 on the expectation that New York would remain the federal capital. Madison and even Washington were censured. In the end, however, the theme of "so what? who cares?" prevailed. The civic improvements occasioned by the residence of Congress might otherwise not have occurred for half a century. When a water route opened to the Great Lakes, the comparatively small city of New York would become the grand emporium of the New World, and the advantages of being the United States capital would pale in comparison to the wealth, grandeur, and influence of New York City.

The First Federal Elections

by Gordon DenBoer

The first federal elections were the essential link between the ratification of the Constitution and the First Federal Congress, which met in March 1789. Political leaders realized that the new federal Constitution provided only a framework for government, and that the first Congress would play a crucial role in giving shape and meaning to the document. Therefore, even before the required ninth state had ratified the Constitution (New Hampshire, on June 21, 1788), both supporters (Federalists) and critics (Antifederalists) of the Constitution began to look ahead and plan for the elections. As George Washington put it for the Federalists on the eve of the elections: ''To be shipwrecked in sight of the Port would be the severest of all possible aggravations to our misery.''

In addition to their political importance, the first federal elections also provided the states with an unusual opportunity to experiment with electoral forms. The Constitution and the Confederation Congress allowed the states wide latitude in choosing senators and in framing their laws for the election of representatives and presidential electors. In conducting the elections, both Federalists and Antifederalists generally supported one electoral method or another, depending on their estimate of how it would affect their chances of winning the elections. The result was a wide diversity in the election laws and in the conduct of the elections.

The Confederation Congress, under the Articles of Confederation, was the nation's supreme constitutional authority from March 1, 1781, until the federal

Congress resolved that the United States be symbolized in a flag of thirteen stripes, alternately red and white, and thirteen white stars on a blue ground. Twelve stars in a circle and one in the center was typical of the period 1777-1795. Courtesy: The New-York Historical Society.

18 government created by the new Constitution went into effect on March 4, 1789. The Confederation Congress was thus responsible for overseeing the ratifications of the Constitution and for making the arrangements for the first federal elections. The Constitution directed that representatives be popularly elected, that the senators be chosen by the state legislatures, and that the presidential electors be chosen ''in such Manner'' as the legislature of each state directed. However, it was Congress' duty to set the time for choosing the electors, the day on which all the electors throughout the country would vote, and the time and place for the first federal Congress to meet. Congress accomplished all of this in its Election Ordinance of September 13, 1788 (the last ordinance passed by the Confederation Congress).

The ordinance required that the electors be chosen on January 7, 1789; that they vote for president and vice president in the respective states on February 4, 1789; and that the First Federal Congress meet in New York City on March 4, 1789. Final passage of the ordinance had been delayed for two months because of the controversy surrounding New York City as the meeting place for Congress. It was generally assumed that the place chosen for the first meeting would influence the choice of a permanent federal capital. Many cities were proposed, but the contest was principally between Philadelphia and New York City, where the Confederation Congress had been meeting since January 1785.

The Constitution's requirement that United States senators be elected by the state legislatures continued the procedure the states had followed since 1776 in electing delegates to the Continental and Confederation congresses. Since many state legislatures were in

session in the fall of 1788 when Congress issued its call for the first federal elections, six states elected their senators before any elections for represenatives were held. Little public attention was generally paid to the choice of senators before they were elected, and only in Massachusetts and New York was there a significant legislative fight over the choices.

In New York, the dispute between the Antifederalist-controlled Assembly and the Federalist-controlled Senate (over the method by which senators and presidential electors should be chosen) was so prolonged that the state did not elect senators until mid-July 1789—four months after the first Congress convened. Federalists Philip Schuyler and Rufus King were finally elected by concurrent resolution of the Assembly and Senate on July 15 and 16. Although Schuyler's election was widely anticipated, the choice of King was a surprise, since he had only recently moved to New York from Massachusetts and was pitted against the better-established James Duane, Lewis Morris, and Ezra L'Hommedieu for the second Senate seat.

Various methods were used by the states to choose presidential electors on January 7, 1789. Delaware, Maryland, Pennsylvania, and Virginia held popular elections; Connecticut, Georgia, and South Carolina used legislative elections; and Massachusetts and New Hampshire used a combination of popular nominations and legislative elections. In New Jersey, the governor and privy council selected the electors. New York failed to elect presidential electors, because of the prolonged quarrel between the Assembly and Senate over how the electors should be chosen, and thus, did not take part in the election of the first president and vice president. North Carolina and Rhode Island

Left: *The New York legislature passed this act on January 27, 1789. It specified the times, places, and manner of electing representatives to the First Federal Congress. Courtesy: New York State Library, Manuscripts and Special Collections Division.* Below: *New York congressional districts, 1789. Courtesy:* The Documentary History of the First Federal Elections.

did not ratify the Constitution until November 21, 1789, and May 29, 1790, respectively, and were consequently ineligible to participate. In most states, the election of electors did not attract widespread attention. The office was, nevertheless, considered an important trust, and the roster of men elected reads like a ''who's who'' of late eighteenth-century United States politicians.

George Washington was the virtually unanimous choice for president, reflecting the widely held assumption that his participation was essential to the successful operation of the new government. Of the candidates mentioned for vice president, only Federalists John Adams, John Hancock, and John Jay were considered serious contenders. Since the president (Washington) would be a southerner, it was generally assumed that the vice president would be from New England. Some Antifederalist support for Governor George Clinton of New York developed, but it quickly evaporated.

The presidential election featured the first use of the Electoral College, one of the Constitution's major innovations. The Constitution directed that each elector vote for two persons; one of whom, at least, could not be a resident of the same state as the elector. The person receiving the most votes would be president (if the votes received were a majority of all the votes cast), while the person with the second most votes would be vice president. Astute contemporary observers saw the flaw in the Constitution's failure to require separate balloting for president and vice president, a flaw which induced some Federalist leaders to manipulate the voting by the electors to ensure that Washington finished ahead of Adams in the balloting. (The Twelfth Amendment to the Constitution, ratified in 1804, re-

quires separate balloting for the two offices.)

In the electoral vote for president on February 4, 1789, Washington received the unanimous support of sixty-nine voting electors, while Adams placed second with thiry-four votes. Jay, with nine votes, and Clinton, with three votes, trailed with eight other also-rans.

Because representatives were popularly elected, those elections attracted far more attention than the selection of senators and presidential electors. In writing the election laws, the major issue in most states was whether to hold statewide elections or to divide the state into districts. Five states (Massachusetts, New York, North Carolina, South Carolina, and Virginia) elected by districts, whereas six states (Connecticut, Georgia, Maryland, New Hampshire, New Jersey, and Pennsylvania) chose statewide elections. Delaware and Rhode Island were each entitled to only one representative.

New York was divided into six districts. Overriding all other issues was the question of whether or not the recently ratified Constitution should be amended. The Antifederalists, who favored amendments, expected to do well in the elections, held March 3-6, 1789. However, the Federalists won in four of the six districts: William Floyd (District 1: Suffolk, Queens, Kings, and Richmond counties); John Laurance, Jr., (District 2: New York City and county, part of Westchester County); Egbert Benson (District 3: Dutchess County and part of Westchester County); and Peter Silvester (District 5: Columbia, Washington and Clinton counties, and the remainder of the state east of the Hudson River). The two Antifederalist victors were John Hathorn (District 4: Ulster and Orange counties) and Jeremiah Van Rensselaer (District 6: Montgomery and Ontario counties,

and Albany County west of the Hudson). The official vote canvass in Albany was not conducted until April 11 (five days after Congress achieved its quorum), and the first New Yorker, John Laurance, Jr., did not take his seat in the House of Representatives until April 8.

Members of Congress, as they gathered in New York City for their first session, were fascinated by the New York political disputes. New York Federalists, meanwhile, were embarrassed by their state's failure to choose presidential electors, by the long delay in electing senators, and by the tardy appearance of their representatives in Congress. Those who favored moving Congress to Philadelphia (or a place further south) were delighted by the squabbling—it strengthened their argument that New York City did not deserve to host Congress.

The First Federal Congress was well into its business by the time the last of the elections were held, and Congress had ultimately to rule on disputed elections for representatives in New Jersey and South Carolina. Nevertheless, the Confederation Congress and the states had skillfully fulfilled their constitutional mandate to conduct the first federal elections.

By the United States in Congress assembled,

S E P T E M B E R 13, 1788.

WHEREAS the Convention aſſembled in Philadelphia, purſuant to the Reſolution of Congreſs of the 21ſt February, 1787, did, on the 17th of September in the ſame year, report to the United States in Congreſs aſſembled, a Conſtitution for the People of the United States; whereupon Congreſs, on the 28th of the ſame September, did reſolve unanimouſly, "That the ſaid report, with the Reſolutions and Letter accompanying the ſame, be tranſmitted to the ſeveral Legiſlatures, in order to be ſubmitted to a Convention of Delegates choſen in each State by the people thereof, in conformity to the Reſolves of the Convention made and provided in that caſe:" And whereas the Conſtitution ſo reported by the Convention, and by Congreſs tranſmitted to the ſeveral Legiſlatures, has been ratified in the manner therein declared to be ſufficient for the eſtabliſhment of the ſame, and ſuch Ratifications duly authenticated have been received by Congreſs, and are filed in the Office of the Secretary--- therefore,

RESOLVED, That the firſt Wedneſday in January next, be the day for appointing Electors in the ſeveral States, which before the ſaid day ſhall have ratified the ſaid Conſtitution; that the firſt Wedneſday in February next, be the day for the Electors to aſſemble in their reſpective States, and vote for a Preſident; and that the firſt Wedneſday in March next, be the time, and the preſent Seat of Congreſs the place for commencing Proceedings under the ſaid Conſtitution.

Cha Thomson ſecy

FOR FURTHER READING

Linda Grant DePauw, *The Eleventh Pillar: New York State and the Federal Constitution.* Ithaca: Cornell University Press, 1966.

John P. Kaminski, "New York: The Reluctant Pillar," in Stephen L. Schechter, ed., *The Reluctant Pillar: New York and the Adoption of the Federal Constitution.* Albany, N.Y.: New York State Bicentennial Commission, 1987.

Staughton Lynd, *Anti-Federalism in Dutchess County, New York.* Chicago: Loyola University Press, 1962.

E. Wilder Spaulding, *New York in the Critical Period, 1783-1789.* New York: Columbia University Press, 1932.

Alfred F. Young, *The Democratic Republicans of New York: The Origins, 1763-1797.* Chapel Hill, N.C.: University of North Carolina Press, 1967.

Confederation Congress' Election Ordinance, September 13, 1788. Signed by Charles Thomson, Secretary of Congress. Courtesy: National Archives.

Setting Precedent:

THE FIRST SESSION OF THE FIRST FEDERAL CONGRESS

by Charlene Bangs Bickford

In New York City, cannons fired, bells pealed, and flags waved, signalling the general joy of the occasion when the appointed day for the convening of the First Federal Congress, March 4, 1789, arrived. The celebrations in New York, which was to host the new legislature, were symbolic of the enthusiasm of the majority of citizens throughout the Union. A letter from New York published in the Portland, Maine, *Cumberland Gazette* describing the festivities expressed this view of the transition:

> *Thus the fourth of March is passing. The old government has gently fallen asleep—and the new one is waking into activity. Let this serve as one instance at least, of people that have power laying it down with pleasure, while they see it with great additions passing into the hands of others.*

New York's preparations for welcoming the new government began in the fall of 1788 when the common council chose architect Pierre L'Enfant to transform the old City Hall into an elegant meeting place for the Congress. L'Enfant and his carpenters were still at work on the building at Wall and Nassau streets when members of the First Federal Congress appeared on March 4. L'Enfant converted the building, which became known as Federal Hall and housed the Congress for its first two sessions, into an outstanding example of early federal architecture and decor.

With only eight senators and thirteen representatives on hand the first day, both houses quickly adjourned, leaving the carpenters to their work. As March passed and no quorum was obtained, the members in attendance, anxious to

Frederick Muhlenberg of Pennsylvania was elected Speaker of the House of Representatives in the First Federal Congress. Oil on canvas by Joseph Wright. Courtesy: National Portrait Gallery, Smithsonian Institution.

begin work, lamented the absence of their colleagues and worried about the image of weakness that was being conveyed to the public. Eventually, on April 6, 1789, a quorum was obtained, and the Congress proceeded to business.

It is almost impossible to exaggerate the importance of the seminal First Federal Congress which, particulary during its first session, acted virtually as a second sitting of the Constitutional Convention, interpreting and providing flesh for the bare-bones structure provided in the Constitution. Its members were well aware of the challenge that lay before them and the need to take quick and decisive action on many fronts. Ratification of the Constitution had been supported by a substantial majority of them, and at the time of their election, only thirteen of the sixty-six men who served in the first House of Representatives and four of the twenty-nine who served in the Senate could be classified as Antifederalists. All but two of the members of this Congress had previously held offices of public trust. Seventeen of them were signers of the Constitution, and most had participated in ratifying conventions. Clearly, they were intensely aware that the success for failure of the new governmental experiment rested upon their shoulders and that, as Connecticut Governor Samuel Huntington reported to Representative Benjamin Huntington, ''Public attention is very much fixed on the proceedings of the new Congress.''

The first session of the First Federal Congress can be characterized as for-

Left: *The first House of Representatives convened at Federal Hall in New York City on April 1, 1789. This desk, designed by Major Pierre Charles L'Enfant, was used by Frederick Muhlenberg of Pennsylvania. Courtesy: The New-York Historical Society.* Right: *Federal Hall, New York City. Meeting place for the First Federal Congress. (From* Massachusetts Magazine, *June 1789.)*

mative. Among its first tasks, each house established the organizational rules by which it would be governed. The House then tackled the creation of a revenue system that would provide a stable source of income to meet the expenses of government. Issues originating from regional and economic differences delayed the passage of this essential act, which set duties on imported goods. Representatives often expressed the view that a particular duty would tax the citizens of their state or

region unfairly or that the infant industrial structure would not be adequately protected. Enactment of the import duties and the system for collecting them came at the end of July.

The long debate over the duties and their collection illustrates that, from its very first meeting, the Congress was required to balance the diverse interests of the eastern, middle, and southern states. As important as any legislation the Congress adopted was the ability of the members to deal with their legis-

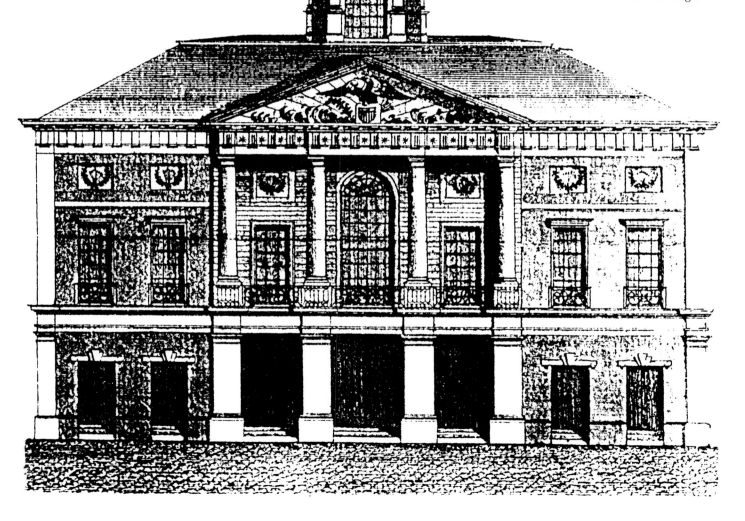

26   lative agenda by transcending their own political compromise, and working to do what was in the nation's interest while representing their constituencies.

The Framers of the Constitution left the job of fleshing out the other two branches of the new government to the Congress. While the Constitution quite explicitly delineated the powers and responsibilities of the Congress and the president, it established no executive departments and left the structure of the federal judiciary largely undefined.

During its first session, the First Federal Congress passed four "organic" acts—laws establishing the state, treasury, and war departments, and the Judiciary Act of 1789. These acts were constitutional in character, even though they were not part of the written Constitution. Therefore, they were subject to alteration or repeal at any time.

By clear implication in the Constitution, the Framers had left the creation of the great departments to Congress. No sooner had Representative Elias Boudinot of New Jersey proposed the creation of such departments than James Madison moved resolutions that proposed that the heads of departments were subject to removal by the president. Madison's resolutions required the Congress to confront and define basic tenets of constitutional interpretation relating to the meaning of separation of powers, advice and consent, and checks and balances.

The questions explored in these debates—who has the power to remove executive officers and how this is accomplished—today seems to us to have

Side chair, ca.1788. Made for Federal Hall in New York City, this chair was used at Washington's Inauguration, April 30, 1789. Courtesy: New York State Museum, Albany. Gift of Wunsch Americana Foundation.
Far Right: Senate Chambers, Federal Hall, 1789. Courtesy: Library of Congress.

28 an easy answer. We are accustomed to the concept that the president has almost complete discretion over the tenure of executive branch officials and to the kind of executive branch that has evolved from the practice. It seems almost unthinkable that anyone would have questioned this presidential power; yet the Constitution is silent on the issue of removal. It left Congress to decide where the authority rested.

During the debate, individual members defended four distinct theories on the removal power. The debate revealed that many interpretations could be advanced in the process of discerning the ''original intent'' of the Founders. William Smith of South Carolina argued that the only method of removal should be that provided for in the Constitution—impeachment, while Theodorick Bland of Virginia was the first to contend that executive officers should be removed in the same manner they were appointed: by the president ''by and with consent of the Senate.'' A majority of the representatives favored removal by the president alone, but were divided as to how the president obtained this power. Was it necessary for the legislature to grant this power to the president or did he already possess this authority implied from the Constitution?

After several days of debate, the implied-power theory was adopted, and all mention of the removal power was eliminated from the legislation. This decision has had a profound impact on the evolution of the federal government. In addition to further defining the relationship between the executive and Congress, it denied the concept of the Senate as a quasi-executive body. Most important for the Federalists, or centralists, who were unwavering supporters of a strong executive, it transferred more power to the executive dur-

Portrait of Senate President John Langdon attributed to Edward Savage, ca.1790. Oil on canvas. Courtesy: Society for the Preservation of New England Antiquities. Photograph by J. David Bohl.

ing George Washington's administration. Washington's unimpeachable reputation made him an invaluable asset to those who were working to achieve what they saw as a true ''balance of power.''

While the House was occupied with the establishment of executive departments and revenue bills, Senate attention was focused on the judiciary bill, legislation fundamental to the history of the development of the judiciary branch. The legislature was granted extensive formulative powers over the judiciary by Article III of the Constitution. Considerable controversy arose during the ratification debates over the role of the third branch of the federal government, and many expressed fears that the federal courts would usurp the judicial rights of the states. Additionally, many of the amendments to the Constitution proposed by the state ratifying conventions sought to put limits on the judicial power and to protect individual rights in federal courts.

Although the Senate elected a committee with a member from each state, the task of drafting the legislation finally fell to a three-member subcommittee. More than any other, Senator Oliver Ellsworth of Connecticut shaped and defended this legislation. In fact, Senator William Maclay in his diary noted that: ''this vile bill is a child of his, and he defends it with the Care of a parent. Even with wrath and anger. He kindled as he always does when it was meddled with.'' This diary provides one of the most colorful, yet complete, eyewitness accounts of the formation of the national government. Ellsworth probably was responsible for the important compromise that allowed for parallel systems of state and federal courts with often concurrent jurisdictions.

The Judiciary Act of 1789, treated elsewhere in this publication, was a masterful legislative achievement. It was so thoroughly and clearly conceived that it was a century before any substantial changes in the judicial system occurred. Ironically, even supporters of the Act, cited by later generations as ''probably the most important and most satisfactory act ever passed by Congress,'' had expected substantial revisions within a few years after its passage.

If twentieth-century Americans were asked to pick the most important accomplishment of the First Federal Congess from a list, the vast majority would select the first ten amendments to the Constitution, the Bill of Rights. Due largely to court decisions, these amendments, together with the Thirteenth, Fourteenth, and Fifteenth, have been utilized to expand rights and protections for individual citizens. *

The significance of the Bill of Rights today would probably surprise members of the First Federal Congress, the majority of whom resisted consideration of amendments to the Constitution when James Madison introduced them. Madison proposed the amendments as a fulfillment of a promise, made during his hard-fought election campaign, thus assuaging Virginia Antifederalists who saw the lack of a bill of rights as a fatal flaw in the Constitution. The majority of the Federalists in Congress, wary of any attempt to alter the governmental structure in the Constitution and believing a federal bill of rights unnecessary, tried to postpone Madison's proposals. As a result of his persistence, twelve amendments were approved by the Congress and sent to the states for ratification. Antifederalists who desired structural amendments believed that they had been betrayed, but the Amendments that were passed, together with trade sanctions, were sufficient to convince reluctant North Carolina and Rhode Island finally to ratify the Constitution.

While much of the credit for the impressive stability of our constitutional system belongs to the Framers, it was the way in which the American people implemented their Constitution that created a functioning system from the document's abstractions. Nothing was more essential to the work of the First Federal Congress. Its achievements were produced by compromise and debate involving people of differing backgrounds, representing diverse regional interests. They faced and resolved many issues that still confront us today: a substantial national debt, sectionalism, the balance of trade, the balance of power between states and the federal government, and the size of the national military establishment. Before the members returned home at the conclusion of the first session, this Congress had begun to grapple with these problems and was evolving into the most important and productive national legislature in American history.

* For a history of the origins and adoption of the Bill of Rights, see *Forgotten Partners: The Bill of Rights and the States*, Stephen L. Schechter, ed. Albany, N.Y.: New York State Bicentennial Commission. Forthcoming.

New York's Delegation in the First Federal Congress

by Charlene Bangs Bickford

On July 16, 1789, the New York legislature ended months of wrangling and debate and appointed two senators to represent the state in the First Federal Congress. Having missed almost four months of the first session, the two men appointed, Rufus King of New York City and General Philip John Schuyler of Albany, presented their credentials to the United States Senate on July 25 and 27, respectively. The political battles resulted in the appointment of two strong supporters of the Constitution and of Federalist programs.

RUFUS KING (1755-1827) was born in Scarboro, Maine, and educated at the Dummer Academy in Massachusetts and at Harvard College. He read law and began practicing in Newburyport, Massachusetts, after being admitted to the bar in 1780. Soon after establishing this practice, he began his distinguished career of public service by representing his town in the Massachusetts General Court. The state legislature sent him to the Confederation Congress, where he served from 1784 to 1787. In the Congress, King was noted for his efforts urging all of the states to contribute toward the maintenance of the government and his attempts to prevent the extension of slavery into the Northwest Territory.

In the period leading up to the Constitutional Convention, King underwent a conversion from his original position opposing radical changes in the Articles of Confederation to become an eloquent supporter of a strong central government. The political unrest in his state, and particularly Shays's Rebellion, caused him to rethink his position and at the Constitutional Convention, he eloquently represented the centralist

Hon. Rufus King, United States Senator from New York. Oil on canvas by Gilbert Stuart. Courtesy: National Portrait Gallery.

viewpoint. After signing the Constitution, he became a principal spokesman for it at the Massachusetts ratifying convention.

During this period, a transition also occured in King's personal life. On March 30, 1786, he married Mary Alsop, thus becoming allied with one of New York City's wealthy merchant families. For nearly three years, King displayed a reluctance to relinquish his influence and position in Massachusetts, but eventually, after making some moves toward running for the Senate from Massachusetts, he decided to make his home in New York. During the long deadlock over the method of choosing senators, Governor Clinton, anxious to prevent control of both seats by the "great and opulent families" and possibly assuming that King could be won over as an ally, sought him out for the Senate appointment. By so doing, Clinton played into the hands of the centralists, for King was already a member of that camp.

King actively participated in the work and deliberations of the Senate, serving on thirty-six committees, including those on the Funding Bill (HR-63), the compensation for the president and vice president, statehood for Vermont, and the first United States census. The only available account of debates in the Senate, Senator William Maclay's diary, reveals that King spoke frequently and was involved in the negotiations leading up to the Compromise of 1790, which resolved the two most difficult issues that the Congress faced—the assumption of the states' Revolutionary War debts and the location of the United States capital. A close associate of Hamilton, he actively supported both the treasury secretary's financial plans and New York as the federal capital. King drew a place in the six-year class in the Senate and was reelected, serving

as one of the ablest Federal senators until his resignation in 1796 to become U.S. Minister to Great Britain.* He was the unsuccessful Federalist candidate for vice president in 1804, and was again elected to the Senate, serving from 1813 to 1825. His last public post was as minister to Great Britain, 1825-1826.

PHILIP SCHUYLER (1733-1804) was born in Albany, attended common schools there, and then studied under a private tutor in New Rochelle. The young heir to extensive lands in the Mohawk and Hudson valleys became a successful farmer, manufacturer, and merchant. In 1755, he married into the Van Rensselaer family of Claverack and joined the British army, where he served as chief commissary. Except for one brief period, he served throughout the French and Indian War, rising to the rank of major. Five years of his service were spent settling colonial claims in England. At the outbreak of the Revolutionary War, his previous military service made him an obvious choice for appointment as one of four major generals immediately under General Washington, and he was put in charge of the Northern Department. After the fall of Ticonderoga in 1777 he was replaced by General Horatio Gates. A court martial, which Schuyler requested, absolved him for the loss of Ticonderoga. He resigned his commission in 1779. Schuyler was a founding member of The Society of The Cincinnati.

Schuyler's political career began with service in the colonial assembly from 1768 to 1776. In 1775, the provincial legislature elected him to the Continental Congress, where he served intermittently during the war (1775, 1777, 1779-1780). He was a state senator from 1780 to 1784 and 1786 to 1790 and a member of the Council of Appointment for four years (1786, 1788, 1790, 1794).

The father-in-law of Alexander Hamilton, Schuyler was the clear choice of the Federalists for the position of United States senator. His election by the legislature was no surprise. While in the Congress, he served on twenty-four committees and reported for ten of them, most of them on matters of finance, Indian affairs, Revolutionary War pensions and compensation, and the military establishment. Maclay identifies Schuyler as one of the major proponents of the Military Establishment Bill (HR-50a), which Maclay calls "the Corner Stone of a Standing Army." Maclay also states that Schuyler was motivated by the "love of Money." Unfortunately for Alexander Hamilton and the other Federalists, Schuyler drew a two-year term and was not reelected. He returned to New York and served in the state senate from 1792 to 1797, when he was reelected to the United States Senate. He served less than a year before resigning due to ill health.

EGBERT BENSON (1746-1833), who represented northern Westchester County and all of Dutchess County, was born in New York City and graduated from Kings (Columbia) College in 1765. After being admitted to the bar in 1769, he practiced in the city and in

Dutchess County, and with his appointment to the provincial legislature in 1775, embarked upon a political career. In 1777, he became a member of the New York Council of Safety, attorney general of the state (a job that he held until 1789), and member of the New York State Assembly (1777-81, 1788). He served in the Confederation Congress (1784, 1787, and 1788), and on the commission to direct the emigration of Tories to loyal British provinces, and also served on several commissions relating to the boundaries of New York State.

Benson, together with Alexander Hamilton, represented New York at the Annapolis Convention in 1786, and a resolution that he later introduced in the New York assembly became the basis for the official action calling a convention to ratify the Constitution. A staunch Federalist, he was defeated for election to that convention.

During the First Federal Congress, his peers appointed him to thirty-six committees. He reported for nine, including panels on the arrangement of the constitutional amendments, titles for the president and vice president, and laws relating to presidential elections and succession. He was an active participant in the debates, speaking on many of the critical issues, particularly the amendments to the Constitution, the acts establishing the executive departments and the judiciary system, and Alexander Hamilton's report on the public credit. Benson was a great admirer of Hamilton and an avid supporter of Federalist programs. He was reelected to the Second Congress.

He served as associate judge of the New York Supreme Court (1794-1801)

Representative William Floyd of Suffolk County. Oil on canvas by Ralph Earl. Courtesy: Independence National Historical Park.

34 and was regent of the University of the State of New York from 1787 to 1802. In 1801, John Adams appointed him chief judge of the U.S. Circuit Court for the Second Circuit, but he lost this position subsequent to the repeal of the 1801 Judiciary Act. He served as the first president of The New-York Historical Society and returned to Congress briefly for a few months in 1813 before resigning from the Thirteenth Congress.

WILLIAM FLOYD (1734-1821), who represented Long Island and Staten Island in the House of Representatives, was born in Brookhaven, Long Island. The son of a wealthy farmer and land-owner, he had little formal education. Upon the death of both parents when he was eighteen, he was thrust into the position of family head and proprietor. A respected member of his community, he risked his fortune and embraced the revolutionary cause in 1774. He joined the Suffolk County militia, where he rose from colonel to major general. New York sent him to the Continental Congress (1774-1777, 1778-1783), and he signed the Declaration of Independence. His career there was un-distinguished, but he was a hard-working and reliable committee member. During this period, Floyd was preoccupied with the fate of his estate, which was endangered during British occupation of Long Island. During the first British attempts to take the island, Floyd led the men who drove them off, but in 1776 his lands were overrun and his family fled to neighboring Connecticut. At the war's conclusion, the estate lay in ruins.

Before his election to the First Federal Congress, Floyd served as a state senator (1777-1783, 1787-1789). His

Egbert Benson represented Westchester and Dutchess counties in the House of Representatives.
Courtesy: Yale University Art Gallery.

election was acceptable to most Federalists and Antifederalists. Once there, he tended to vote with the anti-administration faction, but rarely spoke during debate and clearly was not an advocate for either side. He served on no important committees and did not propose amendments. Floyd was not elected to a second term. Despite his lackluster service in the Congress, this frank and independent man continued to hold public positions, such as that of presidential elector, even after moving to western New York to pioneer at the age of sixty-nine.

JOHN HATHORN (1749-1825), who represented Orange and Ulster counties, began his congressional service on April 23, 1789. A native of Delaware, he completed preparatory studies before becoming a surveyor and schoolteacher. Before the Revolutionary War began, he moved to Warwick in Orange County, where he assisted in surveying the boundary between New York and New Jersey. Appointed to the county militia as a lieutenant colonel when the hostilities began, he rose to the rank of brigadier general in 1786. Hathorn commanded the militia at the battle of Minisink, and tradition holds that attempts on his life were made by a band of Indians and Tories after British General Howe offered a reward. In 1796, he became major general of the state militia. Concurrently, he pursued a political career, serving several terms in the state assembly and for a period as that body's speaker. He was a state senator from 1787 to 1789 and a member of the Council of Appointment in 1787 and 1789. Although he was elected to the Confederation Congress in 1788, he never served.

Like the vast majority of his neighbors and his district's most prominent resident, Governor George Clin-ton, Hathorn was an Antifederalist. Other than the official record of his votes in the Journal of the House of Representatives, there is virtually no available evidence about Hathorn's service in the Congress. No speeches by him were ever reported in the debates, and he was appointed to only one committee. Unfortunately, all of his papers were reportedly destroyed either by a family member or by servants. Although not reelected in 1791, he stood for election to the next three Congresses and was a successful Republican candidate in 1795.

JOHN LAURANCE (1750-1810), who represented New York City and southern Westchester County in the House, emigrated to New York City from Cornwall, England, in 1767. After reading law and being admitted to the bar, he began practicing in the city in 1772. In the First New York Regiment of the Continental Army, he rose from second lieutenant to brigadier general. He then began to put his legal skills to work as judge advocate general on General Washington's staff, a position he held from 1777 to 1782. His political career included membership in the state assembly (1784-85), the Confederation Congress (1785-87), and the state senate (1788-89). He also served as a New York City alderman, 1788-1789. His financial interests flourished from extensive investments in land in New York City and throughout the state.

Everyone expected that New York City would elect a Federalist to the First Federal Congress, but there was a spirited contest for this seat. Laurance was nominated first, but then the merchant interests in the city decided to nominate John Broome. The election hinged on whether a lawyer or a merchant should represent the city. In the end, Laurance won overwhelmingly.

One of the leading defenders of Federalist programs, Laurance spoke on the floor of the House with great frequency and eloquence. His alliance with Alexander Hamilton, one of his partners in land speculation, remained strong throughout his service in the Congress, and he avidly espoused Hamilton's viewpoints and those of other strong nationalists. He served on more than three dozen committees, and was New York's representative in informal negotiations over the location of the capital city. In his diary, Senator William Maclay makes the claim that Laurence held up the presentation of the act to establish a system for collecting duties and tonnage in order to benefit merchants in New York City.

After serving a second term in the House, he returned home and was appointed judge of the U.S. District Court for the District of New York (1794-1796).

From 1796 to 1800, he filled the Senate seat vacated by Rufus King.

PETER SILVESTER (1734-1808), who represented Columbia, Washington, and Clinton counties in addition to Albany County east of the Hudson, was born on Long Island. Subsequent to studying law and being admitted to the bar, he pursued both legal and political careers in Albany. After serving on the Albany Common Council, the Committee of Safety, and the First and Second Provincial Congresses, he moved to the family homestead of his wife, Jannetje Van Schaack, in Kinderhook. There he continued to practice law and served as a judge of the Court of the Common Pleas. He represented Kinderhook in the state assembly in 1788 and was regent of the University of the State of New York for twenty-one years (1787-1808).

The election of Silvester, a Federalist, to the First Federal Congress was the major upset in New York's election for representatives. At the state ratifying convention, his district's delegates were overwhelmingly opposed to the Constitution, but apparently the support of wealthy Federalist landowners was responsible for his victory. He took his seat on April 22, 1789, and although he spoke infrequently during the debates, he did serve on several committees, including those to establish copyright procedures, to create a permanent post of-fice and post roads structure, to authorize appropriations for the year 1790, and to establish a land office in the Northwest Territory. After a second term in Congress, he returned to Kinderhook and served in the state senate (1796-1800) and assembly (1803-1806).

JEREMIAH VAN RENSSELAER (1738-1810), who represented Ontario and Montgomery counties and Albany County west of the Hudson, was born at the family manor house, ''Rensselaerswyck.'' After completing preparatory studies, he studied at private schools in Albany and was graduated from Princeton College in 1758. An heir to the family estate, Van Rensselaer was also a surveyor. He speculated in lands in western New York, including the Dartmouth Township, the Ten Towns, and the Massena Tract. During the early months of the revolutionary movement, he joined both the Albany Sons of Liberty and the Albany Committee of Safety. He served as a paymaster in a New York unit of the Continental Army and was a charter member of The Society of the Cincinnati.

Van Rensselaer actively opposed the ratification of the Constitution, leading the Albany Republican Committee from 1787 to 1789 on behalf of the Antifederalist cause. In 1788 and 1789, he served in the assembly. His district had voted heavily against the Constitution, but his election to the First Federal Congress against Federalist Abraham Ten Broeck was not by an overwhelming margin. Once in the Congress, he was appointed to only five committees, three of those on petitions. There are no reports of any speeches, and no letters that he authored during his congressional service have come to light. He was not reelected, and returned to Albany to serve on the board of directors and as the president of the Bank of Albany and as lieutenant governor of New York (1798-1806).

* United States senators in the First Federal Congress drew lots for two, four, and six-year terms, providing for the election of one-third of the Senate every two years.

Representative Egbert Benson's letter to Samuel Jones, dated December 14, 1790, discussing instructions for New York's congressional delegation. Courtesy: Copley Library, LaJolla, California.

Upon Reflection it has appeared to Me
and I am persuaded it will appear to You,
most advisable that the intended Correspondence
between Us should seem to commence with
You — Indeed it will not be easy for Me or
satisfactory to You for Me to write to You
generally on the Subject, and therefore wish
You would from time to time write to Me
stating the Questions which You may be
desirous to have examined and answered
— It will be most prudent that Your Letters
should be communicated to the other
Gentlemen in the Delegation and therefore
my Answer will in a Degree be public
Communication — I do not purpose
however to confine myself to a mere
Answer to an Interrogatory; my Letters will
contain Suggestions of whatever may occur
to Me as useful. —

We have scarcely entered on the

View of the **TRIUMPHAL ARCH**, *and the manner of receiving General Washington at* Trenton, *on his Route to New-York, April 21.st 1789.*

George Washington's Inaugural Trip to New York

by John P. Riley

With the swearing in of our forty-first president on January 20, 1989, Americans witnessed the pomp and procession that has traditionally graced Inauguration Day for the past two centuries. Yet no celebration of a president-elect's acceptance of this post can match the grandeur that surrounded George Washington's trip to New York in April 1789.

On April 16, 1789, Washington, in a rare diary entry of this period, described his departure from home:

> *About ten o'clock I bade adieu to Mount Vernon, to private life, and to domestic felicity; and with a mind oppressed with more anxious and painful sensations than I have words to express, set out for New York in company with Mr. Charles Thompson, and Colonel Humphries, with the best dispositions to render service to my country in obedience to its call, but with less hope of answering its expectations.*

For the next seven days, Washington would be deluged with honorary dinners, speeches, and revelries at almost every town along the road to New York.

Just nine miles from home, the citizens of Alexandria, Virginia, greeted their favorite son and arranged his first and most memorable stop. This Virginia port knew Washington as early as 1749, when the young surveyor's assistant helped lay out the town's first lots. Forty years later, at a dinner held at Wise's Tavern, Mayor Dennis Ramsay spoke for Washington's long-time neighbors. Ramsay did not praise Washington the soldier nor Washington the president. "Themes less splendid, but more endearing, impress our minds—the first and best of citizens

The scene at Trenton, illustrating George Washington's welcome by the local citizens. Engraving from Columbian Magazine. *Courtesy: Yale University Art Gallery.*

must leave us—Our aged must lose their ornament! Our youth their model! Our agriculture its Improver! Our commerce its Friend…Farewell! Go and make a grateful People happy.…''

Several of his hosts at Wise's Tavern then crossed the Potomac with Washington and his carriage in ferryboats sent from Georgetown, Maryland. From there, Washington and his companions, Secretary of Congress Charles Thomson and former aide-de-camp Davis Humphreys, travelled to Spurrier's Tavern, approximately twelve miles south of Baltimore, Maryland, to spend the night.

Washington was determined to cover the greatest distance possible each day. Some members of Congress had been in New York since March 4, and Washington had promised Senate President John Langdon that he would make speed, keeping in mind the obligatory ceremonies. On the seventeenth, his pledge was tried when ''a large body of respectable citizens on horseback'' conducted Washington, ''under a discharge of cannon, to Mr. Grant's tavern (the Fountain Inn) through crowds of admiring spectators.'' There, the citizens of Baltimore presented an address: ''We behold a new era springing out of our independence, and a field displayed where your talents for governing will not be obscured by the splendor of the greatest military exploits.… We behold, too, an extraordinary thing in the annals of mankind; a free and enlightened people, choosing, by a free election, without one dissenting voice, the late Commander-in-Chief of their armies to watch over and guard their civil rights and privileges.''

The president-elect retired at

10:00 P.M., and the following morning departed at 5:30 amid another burst of artillery fire. On the road to Wilmington, Delaware, Washington turned back ''a body of citizens'' who had accompanied their guest seven miles up the road. ''After thanking them in an affectionate and obliging manner for their politeness,'' Washington insisted that they return home.

Welcoming an uneventful stretch of his journey, Washington spent the night of the eighteenth in the vicinity of Havre de Grace, Maryland. The party reached Wilmington on the evening of the nineteenth and spent a second tranquil night. On the morning of the twentieth, the burgesses and common council of Wilmington welcomed their new leader with several speeches which Washington gratefully received and answered. Boarding their coach, the passengers continued toward Philadelphia. At the Pennsylvania border, a contingent of Philadelphians, mostly Revolutionary War veterans, greeted the former commander in chief. Among these delegates were Thomas Mifflin and Richard Peters, two former members of the Board of War.

Arriving at Chester, Pennsylvania, at 7:00 A.M., Washington enjoyed breakfast among the crowd of early risers. Then, in order to ride in plain view into the streets of Philadelphia, Washington mounted a fine white horse offered him by the city's representatives. Heading the ever-increasing column of wellwishers, Washington turned his steed toward the Schuylkill River. At Gray's Ferry bridge, Washington was surprised by the span ''which was highly decorated with laurel and other evergreens, by Mr. Gray himself, the ingenious [Charles Willson] Peale and others.… At each end there were erected magnificent arches, composed of laurel, emblematic of the an-

cient triumphal arches used by Romans.…'' As Washington passed under the first arch, a young boy dressed in garlands ''let drop, above the Hero's head, unperceived by him, a civic crown of laurel.''

Moving on, Washington led the procession into the city. As cannons fired and churchbells pealed, the citizens of Philadelphia who ''filled the doors, windows, and streets,'' overwhelmed Washington. The *Pennsylvania Gazette* reported that the crowd was ''…greater than on any other occasion we ever remember.'' An elegant dinner prepared at the City Tavern featured a band and fourteen toasts, each followed by a booming of artillery and a quaffing of wine. A local newspaper proclaimed that Washington stayed until the end of the festivities, and ''as usual, captivated every heart.'' He spent the night at the home of his long-time friend, Robert Morris, but before retiring, wrote Senate President Langdon that he would continue his ''journey with as much dispatch as possible. Tomorrow evening I purpose to be at Trenton, the night following at Brunswick and hope to have the pleasure of meeting you at Elizabeth town point (all in New Jersey) on Thursday (April 23) at 12 o'clock.''

Despite the threat of rain on the morning of the twenty-first, Washington endured five separate addresses. To each he offered a brief reply. Insisting that the city troops of horse not escort him to Trenton due to the probability of a

*A nineteenth-century artist's conception of George
Washington's arrival at the Battery in New
York harbor on April 23, 1789. Courtesy: Mount
Vernon Ladies' Association of the Union.*

42 storm, Washington made good time, traversing the west bank of the Delaware.

As Washington approached Trenton, he could not have imagined what her citizens had prepared to honor the hero of January 1777. After taking the lead on a proffered mount, Washington beheld the bridge over Assunpink Creek. An arch of greenery at least twelve feet long and twenty feet high covered the entrance, adorned with the painted phrase, "The Defender of the Mothers will also Defend the Daughters." A large, artificial sunflower topped off the arch.

As he started across the bridge, Washington observed a group of young girls and matrons attired in white who performed a sonata for the general:

Welcome, mighty Chief! once more
Welcome to this grateful shore!

Virgins fair, and Matrons grave,
Those thy conquering arms did save,

Strew, ye fair, his way with Flowers,
Strew your Hero's way with flowers.

As the last lines were sung, girls with baskets of flowers stepped out and scattered blossoms over Washington's path. The moment prompted a correspondent to record that "...the mingled sentiments which crouded into the minds in the moments of solemn stillness during the song, bathed many cheeks with tears." Washington thanked the ladies and proceeded across the bridge, later writing them that they "...have made such impressions on (my) remembrance, as will never be effaced." After enjoying a public dinner and reception at Samuel Henry's City Tavern, Washington spent the night at the home of a Trenton gentleman. At sunrise on the twenty-second, Washington left Trenton behind, breakfasted at Princeton, and took lodgings at Woodbridge, New Jersey.

Before 9:00 A.M. on the twenty-third, Washington reached Elizabeth

Washington entering Gray's Ferry enroute to New York City. Engraving from Columbian Magazine. *Courtesy: Yale University Art Gallery.*

Town where a joint congressional committee escorted him onto a specially prepared barge for the trip to New York City. The vessel, with a keel of forty-seven feet, sported a mast and sail, red curtains, an awning, and thirteen oars on either side. The oarsmen, all New York pilots, wore identical white smocks and black caps. Directed by coxswain Thomas Randall, the barge embarked about noon, moving across Newark Bay and up New York Bay toward the city. An impromptu maritime procession formed as a wide assortment of decorated crafts fell in behind the presidential barge. Upon passing the battery of Staten Island, thirteen guns fired their smoking salutes, directing all the vessels to display their flags. As Washington sailed closer to his destination at the foot of Wall Street, he encountered not only American ships but a Spanish sloop of war, the *Galveston*, and a British packet. The packet fired a thirteen-gun salute, which an American battery answered instantly. The *Galveston* then let loose the first of fifteen cannons, a blast ''so powerful in its detonations'' that it inspired five cheers instead of the customary three huzzahs.

As the barge landed at Murray's Wharf sometime between two and three o'clock, thousands of New Yorkers cheered as Governor George Clinton officially greeted his old acquaintance. Escorted by military guard to Walter Franklin's house at No. 3 Cherry Street, the house hired by Congress for the president's residence, Washington barely had the opportunity to catch his breath when Clinton's carriage arrived to whisk him away to the governor's mansion for an elaborate and extended dinner.

By the time the exhausted guest of honor retired to his new home, visions of this magnificent trip must have raced across his mind. Despite the gushing adulation bestowed upon him almost every step of the way, Washington remained, in fact, humbled and concerned. ''I greatly apprehend,'' he later wrote, ''that my countrymen will expect too much from me. I fear, if the issue of public measures should not correspond with their sanguine expectations, they will turn the extravagant (and I may say undue) praises which they are heaping upon me at this moment, into equally extravagant (though I will fondly hope, unmerited) censures.''

Congress voted to inaugurate Washington on April 30th, a week after Washington's arrival in New York. Time elapsed quickly, as a constant flow of visitors to Cherry Street caused Washington to declare: ''I was unable to attend to any business whatsoever; for Gentlemen, consulting their own convenience rather than mine, were callling from the time I rose from breakfast, often before, until I sat down to dinner.''

On the morning of the thirtieth, Washington dressed in a suit of domestic brown broadcloth, with buttons displaying a wing-spread eagle. White silk stockings, silver shoe buckles and a dress sword resting in a steel scabbard completed his outfit. Numerous representatives conducted the president-elect, alone aboard a decorated coach, to Federal Hall about half past noon and the Inauguration Day ceremonies began.

FOR FURTHER READING 43

James Thomas Flexner, *Washington: The Indispensable Man*. Boston: Little Brown, 1974.

Douglas Southall Freeman, *George Washington: A Biography*. 7 vols. New York: Charles Scribner's Sons. 1948-57.

Barry Schwartz, *George Washington: The Making of an American Symbol*. New York: The Free Press, 1987.

Garry Wills, *Cincinattus: George Washington and the Enlightenment*. Garden City, N.Y.: Doubleday & Company, 1984.

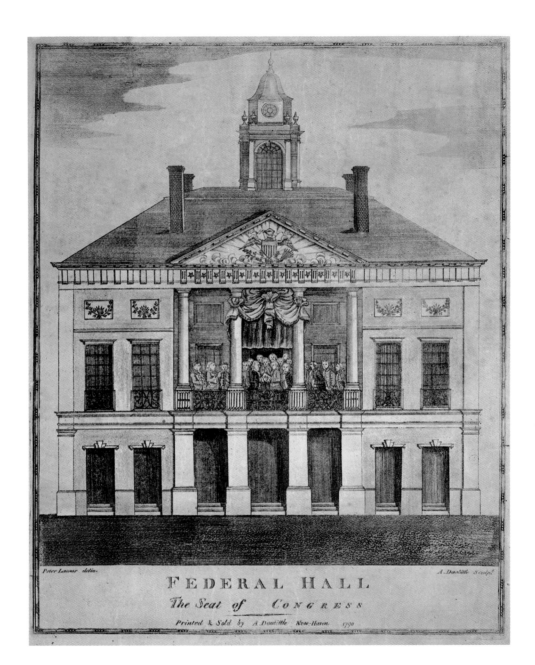

Peter Lacour delin.   A. Doolittle Sculpt.

FEDERAL HALL

The Seat of CONGRESS

Printed & Sold by A. Doolittle New-Haven 1790

The Inauguration of George Washington

by Richard B. Bernstein

This is the great important day.
Goddess of Etiquette assist me
while I describe it.
—Senator William Maclay [1]
Diary, April 30, 1789

April 30, 1789, was supposed to be a great day for the United States of America. It was to be the date on which George Washington would take office as the first president of the United States under the nation's new charter of government, the Constitution of the United States. And, in many ways, the events of that first presidential inauguration were memorable and inspiring. At the same time, however, the first inaugural ceremony was something of a comedy of errors, reflecting the uncertainty plaguing every member of the new government.

The site of the inauguration in New York City, the new republic's first capital under the Constitution, had been ready for weeks. Federal Hall, at the intersection of Wall, Broad, and Nassau streets, was the nation's first capitol building. Formerly old City Hall, the structure had been newly refurbished (the work paid for by private donations raised by such leading New Yorkers as John Jay) under the direction of Major Pierre Charles L'Enfant.

As he waited for news of his election from New York City, the president-elect was by no means sure that he could handle the job—and he was virtually certain that he did not want it. He confided to his friend (and future secretary of war), Henry Knox, that his feelings on going to assume the presidency were "not unlike those of a culprit going to the place of his execution." [2] In fact, even after his election was all but certain, Alexander Hamilton and James Madison had to talk Washington out of a last-minute attack of cold feet. [3] Washington's reluctance grew out of his genuine hope for a peaceful retirement, and his desire to disclaim ambitions

This line etching printed by Amos Doolittle captures the inaugural scene on the balcony of Federal Hall. Courtesy: The Henry Francis du Pont Winterthur Museum.

46 unbecoming a gentleman in assuming public trusts and responsiblities.[4]

Washington and his vice president, John Adams, had been declared elected by the first joint session of the U.S. House of Representatives and the Senate on April 6, 1789. After receiving word of his election from Charles Thomson, the veteran secretary of the old Confederation Congress, Washington left Mount Vernon on April 16 for the journey through Virginia, Maryland, Delaware, Pennsylvania, and New Jersey to New York City. Although he was one of the wealthiest men in the United States, Washington was cash poor, and had to borrow £500 from a neighbor to finance his journey.[5] Martha Washington stayed behind, waiting for word from her husband as to when it would be best for her to join him. Thus, she missed the inauguration on April 30, not arriving in New York City until the end of May.[6]

The trip touched off a week-long bout of patriotic celebration and of adulation for the fifty-seven year-old Virginian. Town after town honored the ''greatest man in the world'' with fetes and ceremonies. On April 23, the president-elect crossed New York Harbor in a large and elaborate barge, rowed by thirteen pilots from the New York Maritime Society. Assorted dignitaries occupied six other barges following the president-elect.[7] The trip across the harbor must have given Washington an uneasy sense of the daunting tasks facing the new government. Although New Yorkers turned out in small sailing boats and along the shore to welcome him, there were no American naval vessels—only a Spanish frigate was on hand to fire a formal salute. Meanwhile, on April 21, John Adams had arrived from Braintree, Massachusetts, uncertain as to what his job was to be and still smart-

ing from the knowledge that he had been elected with one vote less than a majority of the votes cast by the first Electoral College.*

For a week, as Washington waited and conferred with members of the House and Senate, the plans for the inauguration slowly and painfully took shape. The chief stumbling block was the ongoing quarrel between the House and the Senate over questions of protocol. The senators, under the leadership of Vice President Adams, had conceived a passion for titles of office and formal ceremony—a taste not shared by the House of Representatives. The question of titles persisted for weeks after the inauguration. When the Senate proposed such titles for Washington as ''His Elective Highness'' or ''His High Mightiness the President of the United States of America and the Protector of their Liberties,'' the House freezingly pointed out that the Constitution forbade titles of nobility and specified that the chief executive was to be called ''the President of the United States.'' Vice President Adams lamented that there were presidents of fire companies and cricket clubs and predicted that sailors from foreign nations would show no respect for a mere president of the United States and would ''despise him to all eternity.''[8]

As the Senate took the lead in planning the inaugural ceremonies, dazzled by the prospect of creating the equivalent of a republican coronation,

Left: *Oil on canvas portrait of George Washington by James Peale after Charles Willson Peale, ca.1788. This portrait shows the first president of the United States as he looked on April 30, 1789, when he took the oath of office at Federal Hall in New York City. Courtesy: New York Public Library; Astor, Lenox and Tilden Foundations.*
Right: *George Washington's ceremonial sword, believed to have been worn by Washington at the inaugural ceremony: Courtesy: New York State Library.*

Senator William Maclay of Pennsylvania watched sourly. Maclay, a plain-spoken farmer and lawyer, revered Washington; he had protested indignantly against the Senate's taste for titles and ceremony, declaring that Washington needed no titles to be ranked as the first man in the world. Disgusted by his colleague's obsession with ceremony, Maclay began to keep a diary as a record of what he saw and heard and a safe place to confide his acerbic commentary. Newly published in an accurate scholarly edition, the Maclay *Diary* is our principal first-hand account of the inauguration.[9]

On the great day itself, the Senate still had not established the final shape of the ceremonies—or so Vice President Adams maintained. How should the Senate receive the House of Representatives and the new president—standing or sitting? As the senators wasted time and energy batting the question back and forth, the delegation of senators who were to escort Washington to his inauguration forgot to leave, thus delaying the entire ceremony for more than an hour. Finally, the House of Representatives, led by Speaker Frederick A. Muhlenberg of Pennsylvania, marched into the chamber, making much of the discussion academic. They were soon joined by the major participants, George Washington and Chancellor Robert R. Livingston, who had been escorted to Federal Hall by a dignified military procession.

Washington was dressed in a suit of brown broadcloth of American manufacture, to indicate his support for American industries and his belief that he was taking office as a civilian rather than as the former commander in chief of the Continental Army. Because there were as yet no federal judges, Chancellor Robert R. Livingston, the chief

48 judge of the state's equity courts and New York's highest-ranking judge, prepared to administer the oath of office. These men, accompanied by Vice President Adams, Governor George Clinton of New York, and members of the House and Senate, stepped out onto the balcony of Federal Hall.

Crowds of New Yorkers filled Wall, Broad, and Nassau streets. They cheered loudly at their first sight of Washington, and the assembled dignitaries waited for the celebrations to subside. Then Chancellor Livingston and George Washington stepped forward—only to discover that nobody had thought to bring a Bible for the ceremony. A messenger was hastily dispatched to a nearby Masonic lodge to borrow their Bible (Washington and most of the other participants in the ceremony were members of this fraternal order).

Washington repeated the constitutional oath of office after Livingston in a loud, firm voice, ''I do solemnly swear that I will faithfully execute the Office of President of the United States, and will to the best of my Ability, preserve, protect and defend the Constitution of the United States.'' He then added, ''So help me God,'' and bent forward to kiss the Bible. Chancellor Livingston then shouted to the crowd, ''Long live George Washington, President of the United States!'' In so doing, Livingston echoed the traditional cry of welcome for a newly crowned British monarch. The people did not notice this ''trap-

ping of monarchy.'' They gave three cheers, which mingled with the ringing of churchbells and the roar of cannon fired to mark the occasion.

Washington and the other dignitaries then returned to the Senate chamber, where the new president read the first inaugural address in American history. Some controversy exists about the composition of Washington's speech; Irving Brant, James Madison's leading biographer, long maintained that Madison had drafted the speech at his friend's request, but his view has been challenged in recent years.[10]

The substance of the president's speech was clear and simple: Wash-

ington lamented his lack of qualifications, acknowledged and invoked the blessings of Providence, endorsed the new Constitution, and disclaimed any purpose to direct Congress in its legislative responsibilities. In all this, the president was careful to adhere to the prevailing conception of the presidency as a nonpartisan executive office; the president would be the republican equivalent of the king of Great Britain, representing the interests of the whole people of the United States and seeking to advance and protect the general good.[11] Moreover, the president was adhering to the general belief in this period that Congress was the center of

A gilded brass button found at Clermont, the home of Robert R. Livingston. Manufactured for the occasion of the inauguration, its small, 15 millimeter size suggests that it adorned a vest or a coatsleeve. Courtesy: New York State Office of Parks, Recreation and Historic Preservation.
Far right: Chancellor Robert R. Livingston administered the oath of office to George Washington. Oil on canvas by Ezra Ames. Courtesy: Albany Institute of History and Art.

gravity of the constitutional system, and that Congress therefore had the principal responsibility for formulating public policy.[12]

Nonetheless, Washington did choose to comment on one major issue facing the new government—the question of proposed amendments to the Constitution. He knew that the Anti-Federalists had not given up their opposition to the form of government created by the Constitution; rather, they had shifted their ground, seeking by amendment to sap the powers of the new government to regulate commerce and to enact taxes and customs regulations. Moreover, many Anti-Federalists, and indeed many Federalists, had demanded that the Consitution be amended to include a declaration of rights to limit the powers of the government of the United States. The lack of a bill of rights had been the single most powerful argument against the Constitution in the ratification controversy of 1787-1788, and the president was determined, along with Madison and other moderate Federalists, to defuse this objection:

> *Instead of undertaking particular recommendations on this subject, in which I could be guided by no lights derived from official opportunities, I shall again give way to my entire confidence in your discernment and pursuit of the public good: For I assure myself that whilst you carefully avoid every alteration which might endanger the benefits of an United and effective Government, or which ought to await the future lessons of experience, a reverence for the characteristic rights of freemen, and a regard for the public harmony, will sufficiently influence your deliberations on the question how far the former can be more impregnably fortified or the latter be safely and advantageously promoted.[13]*

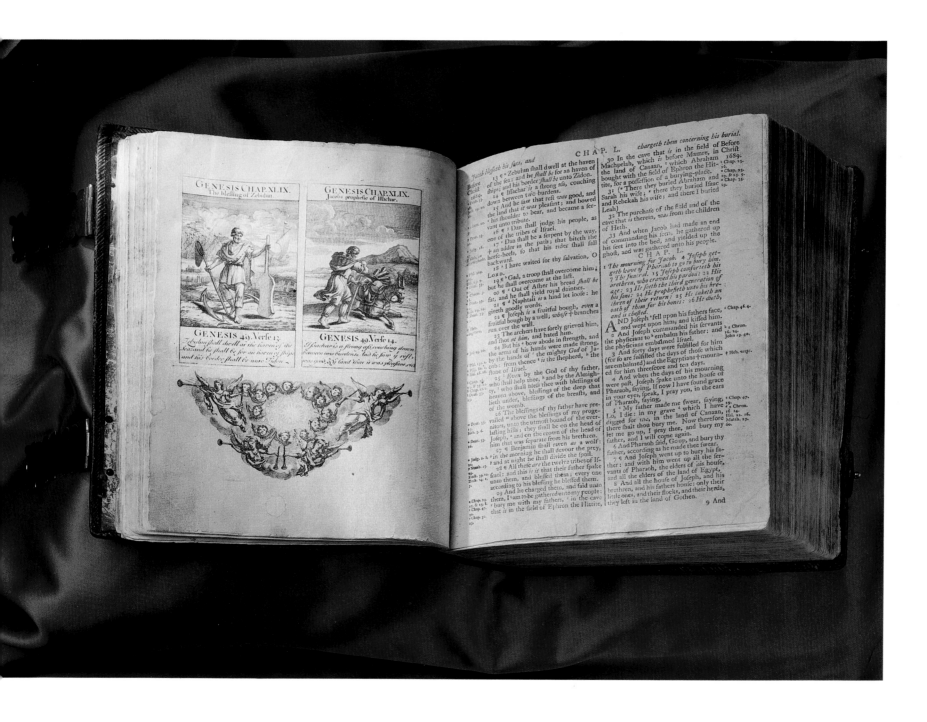

GENESIS CHAP. XLIX.
The blessing of Zebulun.

GENESIS CHAP. XLIX.
Jacobs prophesie of Issachar.

GENESIS 49. Verse 13.
Zebulun shall dwell at the haven of the Sea, and he shall be for an haven of ships; and his border shall be unto Zidon.

GENESIS 49. Verse 14.
Issachar is a strong ass, couching down between two burdens: and he saw that rest was good.

13 ¶ Zebulun shall dwell at the haven of the sea; and he *shall be* for an haven of ships; and his border *shall be* unto Zidon.

14 ¶ Issachar *is* a strong ass, couching down between two burdens.

15 And he saw that rest *was* good, and the land that *it was* pleasant; and bowed his shoulder to bear, and became a servant unto tribute.

16 ¶ Dan shall judge his people, as one of the tribes of Israel.

17 Dan shall be a serpent by the way, an adder in the path, that biteth the horse-heels, so that his rider shall fall backward.

18 I have waited for thy salvation, O LORD.

19 ¶ Gad, a troop shall overcome him: but he shall overcome at the last.

20 ¶ Out of Asher his bread *shall be* fat, and he shall yield royal dainties.

21 ¶ Naphtali *is* a hind let loose: he giveth goodly words.

22 ¶ Joseph *is* a fruitful bough, *even* a fruitful bough by a well, whose branches run over the wall:

23 The archers have sorely grieved him, and shot *at him*, and hated him.

24 But his bow abode in strength, and the arms of his hands were made strong, by the hands of the mighty God of Jacob: from thence *is* the shepherd, the stone of Israel:

25 *Even* by the God of thy father, who shall help thee, and by the Almighty, who shall bless thee with blessings of heaven above, blessings of the deep that lieth under, blessings of the breasts, and of the womb:

26 The blessings of thy father have prevailed above the blessings of my progenitors, unto the utmost bound of the everlasting hills, they shall be on the head of Joseph, and on the crown of the head of him that was separate from his brethren.

27 ¶ Benjamin shall raven *as* a wolf: in the morning he shall devour the prey, and at night he shall divide the spoil.

28 ¶ All these *are* the twelve tribes of Israel: and this *is it* that their father spake unto them, and blessed them; every one according to his blessing he blessed them.

29 And he charged them, and said unto them, I am to be gathered unto my people: bury me with my fathers in the cave that *is* in the field of Ephron the Hittite,

30 In the cave that *is* in the field of Machpelah, which *is* before Mamre, in the land of Canaan, which Abraham bought with the field of Ephron the Hittite, for a possession of a burying-place.

31 (There they buried Abraham and Sarah his wife; there they buried Isaac and Rebekah his wife; and there I buried Leah.)

32 The purchase of the field and of the cave that *is* therein, *was* from the children of Heth.

33 And when Jacob had made an end of commanding his sons, he gathered up his feet into the bed, and yielded up the ghost, and was gathered unto his people.

CHAP. L.

1 *The mourning for Jacob.* 4 *Joseph getteth leave of Pharaoh to go to bury him.* 7 *The funeral.* 15 *Joseph comforteth his brethren, who craved his pardon.* 22 *His age.* 23 *He seeth the third generation of his sons.* 24 *He prophesieth unto his brethren of their return:* 25 *He taketh an oath of them for his bones:* 26 *He dieth, and is chested.*

AND Joseph fell upon his fathers face, and wept upon him, and kissed him.

2 And Joseph commanded his servants the physicians to embalm his father: and the physicians embalmed Israel.

3 And forty days were fulfilled for him (for so are fulfilled the days of those which are embalmed) and the Egyptians mourned for him threescore and ten days.

4 And when the days of his mourning were past, Joseph spake unto the house of Pharaoh, saying, If now I have found grace in your eyes, speak, I pray you, in the ears of Pharaoh, saying,

5 My father made me swear, saying, Lo, I die: in my grave which I have digged for me, in the land of Canaan, there shalt thou bury me. Now therefore let me go up, I pray thee, and bury my father, and I will come again.

6 And Pharaoh said, Go up, and bury thy father, according as he made thee swear.

7 ¶ And Joseph went up to bury his father: and with him went up all the servants of Pharaoh, the elders of his house, and all the elders of the land of Egypt,

8 And all the house of Joseph, and his brethren, and his fathers house: only their little ones, and their flocks, and their herds, they left in the land of Goshen.

9 And

Washington then refused any salary, expressing the hope that Congress simply would consent to pay his expenses, as the Continental Congress had done when he accepted the office of commander in chief of the Continental Army in 1775. Perhaps remembering the staggering total at the end of Washington's detailed 1775-1783 expense account, Congress persisted in adopting a presidential salary. [14]

Although the substance of Washington's speech was guaranteed to win the approval of Congress, his delivery surprised and pained his audience. William Maclay has left us the best eyewitness account:

[T]his great Man was agitated and embarrassed more than ever he was by the levelled Cannon or pointed Musket. He trembled, and several times could scarce make out to read, though it must be supposed he had often read it before. He put part of the fingers of his left hand, into the side, of what I think the Taylors call the fall, of his Breeches. Changing the paper into his left hand, after some time, he then did the same with some of the fingers of his right hand. When he came to the Words all the World, *he made a flourish with his right hand, which left rather an ungainly impression. I sincerely, for my part, wished all set ceremony in the hands of the dancing Masters, and that this first of Men, had read off, his address, in the plainest Manner without ever taking his Eyes From the paper, for I felt hurt, that he was not first in everything.* [15]

After the president finished his speech, he and the House and Senate adjourned to nearby St. Paul's Chapel

George Washington took the oath of office with one hand placed on this Bible, borrowed for the occasion from St. John's Lodge, Free and Accepted Masons. Courtesy: LIFE Magazine, c.1989. Time, Inc. Photo by Martha Stanitz

for a religious service; Maclay had recorded his discontent at this proposal, blaming the "churchmen" (that is, Episcopalians) in the Senate. [16] That evening, the finest display of fireworks and illuminations yet seen in the United States took place in New York City to celebrate the launching of the new government.

*See Gordon DenBoer, *The First Federal Elections,* elsewhere in this publication.

[1]Kenneth Bowling and Helen Veit, eds., *The Diary of William Maclay and Other Notes of Senate Debates* (vol. IX, *Documentary History of the First Federal Congress*) (Baltimore: Johns Hopkins University Press, 1988), 11 (entry for April 30, 1789) (Hereafter Maclay, *Diary*).

[2]George Washington to Henry Knox, April 1, 1789, quoted in Clarence W. Bowen, ed., *History of the Centennial of the Inauguration of George Washington as First President of the United States* (New York: Lippincott, 1892), 21.

[3]See the discussion in Bowen, ed., *Centennial History*, 21.

[4]See generally Garry Wills, *Cincinnatus: George Washington and the Enlightenment* (New York: Doubleday, 1984); Barry Schwartz, *George Washington: The Making of an American Symbol* (New York: Free Press/Macmillan, 1987).

W.B. Allen has prepared a valuable one-volume selection of Washington's writings. W.B. Allen, ed., *George Washington: A Collection* (Indianapolis: Liberty Press/Liberty Classics, 1988).

[5]George Washington to Captain Richard Conway, March 4 and 6, 1789, quoted in Bowen, ed., *Centennial History*, 21.

[6]Elizabeth McCaughey, *Government by Choice: Inventing the U.S. Constitution* (New York: Basic Books/The New-York Historical Society, 1987), 113.

[7]Bowen, ed., *Centennial History*, 28-34.

[8]Maclay, *Diary*, 31 (entry for May 9, 1789).

[9]Kenneth Bowling's and Helen Veit's Introduction (Maclay, *Diary*, xi-xvii) and biographical sketch (Appendix E in *id.*, 431-445) are our best accounts of Maclay's life, the circumstances which prompted him to begin his *Diary*, and its historiographical significance.

[10]*Washington's Inaugural Address of 1789* (Washington: National Archives and Records Administration, 1986), 4-5.

[11]See Ralph Ketcham, *Presidents Above Party: The First American Presidency, 1789-1829* (Chapel Hill, N.C.: University of North Carolina Press, 1984).

[12]This discussion is based upon the writer's work-in-progress, Richard B. Bernstein, "'Conven'd in Firm Debate': The Development of the House of Representatives as an Instrument of Republican Government, 1789-1791." See also Richard B. Bernstein with Kym S. Rice, *Are We to Be a Nation?* (Cambridge, Mass.: Harvard University Press, 1987), 246-249.

[13]Quoted in Bernstein with Rice, *Are We to Be a Nation?*, 263.

[14]See Gen. George Washington and Marvin Kitman, PFC (Ret.), *George Washington's Expense Account* (New York: Simon & Schuster, 1970).

[15]Maclay, *Diary*, 13 (entry for April 30, 1789).

[16]*Id.*, 8 (entry for April 27, 1789).

FOR FURTHER READING

W.B. Allen, ed., *George Washington: A Collection.* Indianapolis: Liberty Press/Liberty Classics, 1988.

Richard B. Bernstein with Kym S. Rice, *Are We to Be a Nation? The Making of the Constitution.* Cambridge, Mass.: Harvard University Press, 1987.

James D. Hart, *The American Presidency in Action: 1789.* New York: Macmillan, 1948.

Ralph Ketcham, *Presidents Above Party: The First American Presidency, 1789-1829.* Chapel Hill, N.C.: University of North Carolina Press, 1984.

Forrest McDonald, *The Presidency of George Washington.* Lawrence: University Press of Kansas, 1974.

John C. Miller, *The Federalist Era, 1789-1801.* New York: Harper & Row, 1960.

Leonard D. White, *The Federalists: A Study in Administrative History.* New York: Macmillan, 1948.

"I Walk on Untrodden Ground:"

GEORGE WASHINGTON AS PRESIDENT, 1789-1797

by Richard B. Bernstein

President George Washington found it difficult to share the feelings of joy and pride that prevailed at his inauguration in 1789. He knew the magnitude of the task before him. He wrote, ''Few who are not philosophical spectators can realize the difficult and delicate part which a man in my situation had to act....I walk on untrodden ground. There is scarcely any part of my conduct which may not hereafter be drawn into precedent.''[1]

As Washington knew, the presidency of the United States was unique in the history of government. Its creation caused the Framers of the Constitution as much trouble as anything else in the document. As the presidency took shape at the Federal Convention in the summer and fall of 1787, the few dozen men who struggled to define the office found themselves under the shadow of two Georges: George III and George Washington.[2]

The Framers of the Constitution were wrestling with the concept of executive power, which most Americans had learned to distrust in the revolutionary era.[3] In the years leading up to the American Revolution, British and American advocates of the colonists' cause repeatedly appealed to George III as an impartial ''patriot king'' who could mediate among his subjects to achieve the common good. The Americans bitterly resented King George's failure even to acknowledge their arguments; they also resented his representatives in America, the royal governors of the colonies. Thus, most state constitutions framed during the

The Whiskey Rebellion prompted George Washington to don his military uniform once more. This scene depicts Washington reviewing the western army at Fort Cumberland, Maryland. Oil on canvas by Kemmelmeyer. Courtesy: The Metropolitan Museum of Art, gift of Edgar William and Bernice Chrysler Garbisch, 1963.

1770s had cut back sharply on the authority and independence of their chief executives, or governors, and Pennsylvania and Vermont had done away with an independent executive altogether.[3]

At the same time, American political thinkers such as John Adams of Massachusetts, John Jay of New York, and Thomas Jefferson of Virginia counseled against abandoning executive power altogether. The New York constitution of 1777 (largely the work of Jay), the Massachusetts constitution of 1780 (drafted by Adams), and Jefferson's criticisms of the Virginia constitution of 1776 found a wide and appreciative audience, and shaped the thinking of those who framed the U.S. Constitution a decade later.

Equally important in the creation of the presidency was Washington's presence at the Federal Convention as a Virginia delegate. As he presided over the convention's debates, he may well have been aware of his fellow delegates' appraising glances. If the proposed Constitution was adopted, its Framers thought, Washington most likely would be the first man chosen to be president; for this reason, the aged Benjamin Franklin urged, they need not give in to their fears as they shaped the office. Washington's shadow, too, hung over the Convention, as the delegates sought to strike a balance between their hopes, symbolized by Washington, and their fears, symbolized by George III.

Washington already had had a great deal of practice as the repository of his fellow citizens' confidence.[4] Ever since 1775, when he was named commander in chief of the Continental Army, Washington had been a living symbol of the Revolution, independence, and American nationalism. Throughout the war, he had to watch his conduct lest any slip or indiscretion on his part

damage his country's cause. Even in peace, the general kept a sharp eye on the propriety of his public and private life. He worried lest his service as a delegate to the Federal Convention in 1787 be seen as betraying his 1783 pledge that he was done with public affairs. He remained silent during the ratification controversy, content to let his signature on the Constitution speak for itself. And, when it became all but certain that he would be chosen as the first president of the United States, his friends and supporters, James Madison and Alexander Hamilton, had constantly to reassure him that it was appropriate for him to accept the office.

Thus, the first president was already familiar with, if not sensitive to, one of the most difficult tasks confronting any president; namely, that of Head of State. Although he often found his symbolic role painful and embarrassing, Washington gamely bore the burden. In his conduct as president, Washington sought to maintain his personal dignity and reserve in the hope that it would come to be associated with the office he held, so that the personal respect he enjoyed would also attach itself to the presidency. In particular, he followed the advice of his longtime advisor Alexander Hamilton who maintained that pomp and ceremony were necessary to preserve the respect of the people for their chief executive. Other Americans, worried lest the people forget that they had once overthrown a monarch, repeatedly criticized Washington for assuming kingly airs and for condoning

the ornate ceremony of formal receptions, or *levees*.

This symbolic role dominated the president's first year in office. He had little else to do except to sign bills enacted by Congress and to fill offices created by Congress. He found this last responsibility especially burdensome. As he explained to one friend:

That part of the President's duty which obliges him to nominate persons for offices is the most delicate and in many instances will be, to me, the most unpleasing, for it may frequently happen that there will be several applicants for the same office, whose merits and pretensions are so nearly equal that it will almost require the aid of supernatural intuition to fix upon the right.[5]

Washington governed his appointments' policy by reference to three criteria. First, he sought the ablest men available. Second, he preferred to appoint those whom he knew to be warm friends of the Constitution and sincerely committed to its success. Third, aware of the touchy sensibilities of the several states and sections of the United States, he strove for geographic balance in his appointments to national office.

As discussed elsewhere in this book, Washington devoted great care to selecting his principal advisers, the heads of the executive departments created by Congress. He regarded as a mandate of his office the part of Article II, Section 2 of the Constitution authorizing the president to require the written opinions of the heads of the executive departments on major questions, and convened them regularly to discuss pending issues. This practice gave rise to the first major extra-constitutional institution, the president's Cabinet (a term borrowed from British usage). In addition to his Cabinet members, the president also consulted Representative James

Madison of Virginia (on whom he had come to rely during the adoption of the Constitution) and Chief Justice John Jay.

Washington's habit of seeking advice from all available sources became a sore point with his critics, who charged that he was indecisive. A more accurate assessment came from his first secretary of state, Thomas Jefferson, who declared long after Washington's death that the president's mind was ''slow in operation, being little aided by invention or imagination, but sure in conclusion.''[5]

Washington's practice of seeking advice from as many sources as possible occasionally had constitutional consequences. At one point in his first term, Washington and Jefferson inadvertently set a major precedent in the area of separation of powers. They sought to submit a question of treaty interpretation to the Supreme Court, seeking what we would call an ''advisory opinion.'' The justices politely but firmly refused, declaring that their powers extended only to actual ''cases or controversies,'' as required by Article III of the Constitution. Similarly, when Washington and Secretary of War Henry Knox sought the advice and consent of the Senate to a proposed strategy for negotiating a treaty with Indian tribes, the embarrassed U.S. senators suggested that the president return when he had a completed treaty to lay before them. This incident established the understanding that negotiating a treaty falls within the province of the executive branch, with the Senate's role limited to ratifying or rejecting all or part of what the executive had been able to negotiate.

John Adams's term as vice president was not a happy one—for eight years he languished beneath the shadow of George Washington. Courtesy: Independence National Historical Park.

President Washington tended to defer to Congress in the shaping of federal policy, exercising his veto power only when he believed a proposed statute to be unconstitutional. As to economic issues, he permitted Treasury Secretary Hamilton great discretion, largely due to his confidence in Hamilton's knowledge and ability. On the other hand, he acted as his own secretaries of state and war, believing that he had adequate experience and knowledge to assume these responsibilities. This tendency caused few problems for Secretary Knox, who resumed the familiar habit of executing Washington's instructions as he had done during the Revolution. However, Thomas Jefferson, one of the nation's most experienced diplomats, chafed at the degree to which, as secretary of state, he was forced to follow the dictates of the president rather than have a free hand in shaping policy.[7]

The most important instance of Washington's practice of directing foreign relations came in 1793. With Europe convulsed by a war between the revolutionary French Republic and the conservative monarchies, pressure mounted on the United States to take sides. Supporters of the French, including Secretary of State Jefferson and Representative Madison, maintained that the 1778 friendship treaty between France and the United States required the United States to come to the aid of its old ally. Those who distrusted and feared the revolutionary French government, such as Treasury Secretary Hamilton, Secretary of War Knox, Vice President Adams, and Chief Justice Jay, maintained that the United States should remain neutral, and that the 1778 treaty had been abrogated by the overthrow of the former French monarchy. Washington ultimately accepted the arguments for neutrality, issuing a Neutrality Proclamation and, by implication, asserting inherent presidential authority over foreign relations.[8]

Few men could have managed to hold together a Cabinet containing members as brilliant and antithetical as Hamilton and Jefferson. More than once, the president had to resort to cajolery and even to formal reprimands to control the antagonism that threatened to split his government. He tended to sympathize with Hamilton's point of view, for he shared with Hamilton first-hand knowledge of the weaknesses that had nearly destroyed the United States under the Articles of Confederation, as well as a pessimism about human nature lurking just underneath the calm face he showed to the world. When Jefferson left the Cabinet in 1793, soon after he had joined forces with Hamilton to persuade the president to accept a second term, Washington was hurt by what he saw as Jefferson's betrayal and, in consequence, placed even more reliance on Hamilton and the Federalists.

Nonetheless, Washington was alarmed by the rivalry and dissension between Hamilton and Jefferson, for it hinted at an even more ominous development in the nation-at-large—the rebirth of party strife.[9] Washington viewed the growing rupture between his administration's supporters, or Federalists, and opponents, or Republicans, as the first signs of factional strife that might tear the republic to pieces. This had been the teaching of political philosophers and historians of republican government for thousands of years, and virtually every leading member of the revolutionary generation shared these views. Despite their fears, however, the American political system adapted to the development of political parties, and the Republic did not fall.

Yet another presidential role inaugurated by the first president was that of commander in chief of the armed forces, a role specified in the Constitution. In 1794, it became apparent that the farmers of western Pennsylvania were refusing to pay federal taxes on whiskey, an important element of Hamilton's fiscal program. Hamilton was outraged by this defiance of federal authority, and the president agreed. Washington placed the militias of Pennsylvania, New Jersey, Maryland, and Virginia under federal authority, and became the first of only two presidents actually to take the field as commander in chief. He, Hamilton, and General Henry Lee led an army of 12,500 men throughout western Pennsylvania seeking the rebels. Although the ''Whiskey Rebellion'' turned out to be more rumor than reality, Washington's actions vindicated the authority of the federal government. They also alarmed Republicans, who feared that the army might be used to suppress them even though the First Amendment protected their political rights.[10]

Seeking to ease the tension between Great Britain and the United States, Washington sent Chief Justice John Jay to London to negotiate a treaty. Jay's instructions, which again provoked heated dissensions within the Cabinet,

were wide ranging, granting the veteran diplomat great discretion and authorizing him to take account of border disputes, the question of unpaid debts to British creditors, and trade issues. When Jay returned from London with a treaty in hand, its terms seemed so one-sided in favor of Britain that even Jay's friend Hamilton was startled. The dispute over the Jay Treaty exacerbated the already tense situation in American politics. Republican gatherings hanged Jay in effigy; one outraged opponent of the treaty wrote, "Damn John Jay! Damn everyone who won't damn John Jay! Damn everyone who won't sit up all night with a candle in his window damning John Jay!" Despite all odds, the Senate ratified the treaty. The Republican-dominated House sought to impede putting the treaty into effect, invoking its authority over appropriations as justification, but Washington resisted the House's actions as violating the separation of powers, and ultimately prevailed.[11]

In 1796, Washington determined to retire at the end of his second term. He had lost all his closest advisors to retirement, and he had had given up any hope of securing a Cabinet representing diverse points of view. His new Cabinet was composed of second-rate men who were firm Federalists, and the president often gave in to outbursts of temper against Republican opposition to his administration. He bitterly regretted having been persuaded to accept a second four-year term, and yearned for the peace and tranquility of Mount Vernon. He turned once more to Hamilton, asking him to prepare a farewell address. Washington then carefully reworked

George Washington (at right) and his first Cabinet: Henry Knox, seated; Thomas Jefferson, Edmund Randolph (his back to the artist), and Alexander Hamilton. Courtesy: The New-York Historical Society.

58 Hamilton's draft, line by line, to put it in his own words and emphasize the points he wanted stressed. Further drafts went back and forth between New York and Philadelphia until the president was satisfied.

On September 19, 1776, the Farewell Address was published in David C. Claypoole's *American Daily Advertiser*. This statement, the capstone of Washington's political writings, is remembered today for its eloquent advice against entangling alliances with foreign nations. An equally important theme of his address was Washington's denunciation of the spirit of party and factionalism which, he warned, could still destroy the fragile American experiment in government. These passages of the address provoked Republican hostility, for members of the opposition rightly felt that the president was singling them out for blame for the rise of party controversy. Read out of context, the Farewell Address may well appear as a disinterested valedictory, but when the reader recalls that it appeared in the middle of the 1796 presidential campaign, the address looks more and more like a Federalist campaign document. By this point, the retiring president had so gone over to the Federalist camp that he could not perceive his party bias.

On March 4, 1797, as Washington congratulated his successor, John Adams, the new president had a curious fancy, which he confided in a letter to his wife, Abigail. ''Ay!'' the ex-president seemed to say, ''I am fairly out and you are fairly in. See which of us will be happiest.''[13] It was clear that the former president was overjoyed to have relinquished the burden of office. For the first time in more than two

Secretary of the Treasury Alexander Hamilton. Oil on canvas by John Trumbull. Courtesy: Yale University Art Gallery.

decades, he could think of himself as a purely private citizen. If he pondered the preceding eight years, with all their frustrations, he could take pride in knowing that he had done all he could to ensure that the new government was successfully launched. Fifteen years after Washington's death in 1799, his old adviser and adversary Thomas Jefferson penned what may well be the most fitting summation of Washington's career:

His was the singular destiny and merit of leading the armies of his country successfully through an arduous war for the establishment of its independence, of conducting its councils through the birth of a government, new in its forms and principles, until it settled down into a quiet and orderly train; and of scrupulously obeying the laws through the whole of his career, civil and military, of which the history of the world furnishes no other example.[13]

[1] Quoted in Robert F. Jones, *George Washington,* rev. ed (New York: Rose Hill Books/Fordham University Press, 1986), 88.

[2] This metaphor comes from Richard B. Bernstein and Jerome Agel, *Into the Third Century: The Presidency* (New York: Walker, 1989), Ch. 1.

[3] Willi Paul Adams, *The First American Constitutions* (Chapel Hill, N.C.: University of North Carolina Press, 1980). See also Ralph Ketcham, *Presidents Above Party: The First American Presidency, 1789-1829* (Chapel Hill, N.C.: University of North Carolina Press, 1984).

[4] See generally Barry Schwartz, *George Washington: The Making of an American Symbol* (New York: Free Press, 1987); Paul K. Longmore, *The Invention of George Washington* (Berkeley: University of California Press, 1988); Garry Wills, *Cincinnatus: George Washington and the Enlightenment* (New York: Doubleday, 1984).

[5] George Washington to Joseph Jones, May 14, 1789, quoted in Richard B. Bernstein with Kym S. Rice, *Are We to Be a Nation? The Making of the Constitution* (Cambridge, Mass: Harvard University Press, 1987), 245.

[6] Thomas Jefferson to Walter Jones, January 2, 1814, quoted in Jones, *George Washington,* 159.

[7] Forrest McDonald, *The Presidency of George Washington* (1974; New York: W.W. Norton, 1975), 40-41.

[8] McDonald, *Presidency of Washington,* 125-127; John C. Miller, *The Federalist Era, 1789-1801* (New York: Harper & Row, 1960), 128-139.

[9] The literature on the origins of parties is enormous. See generally Richard Hofstadter, *The Idea of a Party System* (Berkeley: University of California Press, 1969); Joseph Charles, *Origins of the American Party System* (1955; New York: Harper & Row, 1963); Miller, *Federalist Era, passim;* Kenneth R. Bowling, ''Politics in the First Congress, 1789-1791'' (unpublished Ph.D. dissertation, University of Wisconsin, Madison, 1968); and the sources cited in Bernstein with Rice, *Are We to Be a Nation?,* 318 n. 26.

[10] See generally Steven Boyd, ed., *The Whiskey Rebellion* (Westport, Conn.: Greenwood Press, 1985); Thomas Slaughter, *The Whiskey Rebellion* (New York: Oxford University Press, 1986).

[11] On the diplomatic background and context of Jay's mission, the classic study is Samuel Flagg Bemis, *Jay's Treaty,* rev. ed (New Haven: Yale University Press, 1960). On the political controversy, see Jerald A. Combs, *The Jay Treaty* (Berkeley: University of California Press, 1970); Charles, *Origins,* Ch. 3.

[12] John Adams to Abigail Adams, March 5, 1797, quoted in Jones, *George Washington,* 139.

[13] Thomas Jefferson to Walter Jones, January 2, 1814, quoted in Jones, *George Washington,* 161.

James Thomas Flexner, *George Washington.* 4 vols. Boston: Little, Brown & Co., 1963-1973. (One-volume abridgment: James Thomas Flexner, *Washington: The Indispensable Man.* Boston: Little, Brown & Co., 1975).

James Hart, *The American Presidency in Action: 1789.* New York: The Macmillan Company, 1948.

Ralph Ketcham, *Presidents Above Party: The First American Presidency, 1789-1829.* Chapel Hill, N.C.: University of North Carolina Press, 1984.

Robert P. Jones, *George Washington.* Originally published, New York: Twayne, 1979; rev. ed., New York: Rose Hill Books/Fordham University Press, 1986.

Forrest McDonald, *The Presidency of George Washington.* Originally published Lawrence, Kansas, University Press of Kansas, 1974; New York: W.W. Norton & Company, 1975.

John C. Miller, *The Federalist Era, 1789-1801.* New York: Harper & Row, 1960.

Leonard D. White, *The Federalists: A Study in Administrative History.* New York: The Macmillan Company, 1948.

The "Great Departments":

THE ORIGIN OF THE FEDERAL GOVERNMENT'S EXECUTIVE BRANCH

by Richard Allan Baker

In its first years, the executive branch of the federal government consisted essentially of the president and his three principal advisers—a modest beginning. Among these advisers—the secretaries of treasury, state, and war—Treasury Secretary Alexander Hamilton ranked first, combining superior administrative skills with a sparkling intellect. Secretary of State Thomas Jefferson, who would rather have remained minister to France, took secondary place in this exclusive company. And the congenial Henry Knox, preoccupied with his wife's gambling debts, served without noticeable distinction as secretary of war. Playing significant supporting roles, but apart from these chiefs of the "Great Departments," were Postmaster General Samuel Osgood and Attorney General Edmund Randolph.

At the 1787 Constitutional Convention, delegates demonstrated little interest in the specifics of executive department organization. Once they had determined the powers and responsibilities of the presidential office, they simply assumed that an adminstrative structure would form to continue the basic governmental functions of finance, foreign relations, and defense that existed under the Articles of Confederation. The Constitution's only explicit reference to this structure appears in Article II, Section 2 with the provision that the president "... may require the opinion, in writing, of the principal officer in each of the executive departments, upon any subject relating to the duties of their respective offices...."

For several months after George Washington took his oath of office on April 30, 1789, he served as virtually the entire executive branch. Caretakers left

George Washington. Oil on canvas by Rembrandt Peale, 1853. Courtesy: The New-York Historical Society.

over from the Confederation government awaited presidential and congressional initiative: John Jay as secretary for foreign affairs, Henry Knox as secretary of war and Samuel Osgood, who looked after the country's post offices. The old Treasury Board continued to manage the nation's finances.

On June 8, 1789, while waiting for Congress to pass legislation establishing the three major departments, Washington asked each of the acting secretaries for a written survey of the "real situation" within their agencies. He urged them to provide a "clear account...as may be sufficient (without overburdening or confusing the mind which has very many objects to claim its attention at the same instant) to impress me with a full, precise, and distinct general idea of the affairs of the United States, so far as they are comprehended in, or connected with that department."

In his relations with the embryonic executive departments, President Washington proved to be a capable adminstrator. His military command and staff experience became apparent in his manner of reviewing proposals of subordinates, in outlining plans for them to expand, and in his pursuit of opinions regarding the constitutionality of legislation and policy decisions. Thomas Jefferson later described Washington's managerial style: "If a doubt of any importance arose," wrote Jefferson, the president "reserved it for conference. By this means, he was always in accurate possession of all facts and proceedings in every part of the Union, and to whatsoever department they related; he formed a central point for the different branches; preserved a unity of object and action among them; exercised that participation in the suggestion of affairs which his office made incumbent upon him; and met himself the due responsibility for whatever was done."

Initially, Washington consulted with his department heads, individually or collectively, as circumstances dictated. Within four years, however, this group began to meet regularly and became known as the president's "Cabinet." He worked with his senior officers during the Revolutionary War, often changing his own plan in the face of adverse opinion from his advisers. In the early years, the president encouraged opposing views, and he got them in abundance in bitter clashes between Secretary of State Thomas Jefferson and Treasury Secretary Alexander Hamilton. By 1793, as the burdens of the presidency increased, Washington concluded that henceforth he would avoid advisers "whose political tenets are adverse to the measures which the general government are pursuing."

THE TREASURY DEPARTMENT

The statute creating the Treasury Department contained greater detail than those establishing the departments of state and war, yet all three were remarkably brief. Treasury was the largest of the three cabinet agencies and, during the early years of the new government's existence, it grew at a faster rate than the other two. Congress singled out that agency for special attention by providing a direct tie between it and the legislature. Unlike the heads of the other two departments, who were to carry out their duties "in such manner as the President of the United States shall, from time to time order or instruct," the treasury secretary was given

a specific congressional mandate. The statute provided that he "digest and prepare plans for the improvement and management of the revenue, and for the support of the public credit" and that he "make report, and give information to either branch of the legislature, in person or in writing... respecting all matters referred to him by the Senate or House of Representatives, or which shall appertain to his office." The act contained no explicit provision for presidential supervision of the secretary. Six days after Hamilton became treasury secretary, the House of Representatives abolished its Committee on Ways and Means. This action suggested that the House intended the secretary to take the initiative in the formulation and implementation of general financial policy: preparing revenue measures, drafting public reports, managing financial operations, and placing public funds in banks and other financial institutions.

Even before the department was officially established, Congress assigned it operational control of the customs service, lighthouses, and sailing vessel registration. Beyond its intitial financial duties, the department soon acquired responsibility for administering a $12 million loan for conducting land surveys. Customs collectors took on the additional tasks of paying military pensions and purchasing army supplies.

The department's large number of employees reflected its broad responsibilities. At the end of 1789, its central office included six chief officers, three principal clerks, twenty-eight clerks, and two messengers. Within a year, that number had nearly doubled. By 1801, the Treasury Department employed more than half of all federal government workers, including a field staff of 1,600 revenue collectors.

The combination of Alexander Hamilton's leadership and the Treasury Department's vital function in raising revenue made that agency preeminent. Hamilton had actively campaigned for the position well in advance of his September 1789 appointment. While many friends urged him to avoid the Treasury—with the nation's finances in a ''deep, dark, and dreary chaos''—and run for the Senate, or seek nomination as chief justice of the U.S. Supreme Court, Hamilton believed that he was one of the few men available who possessed the training and experience to accomplish this difficult task. When Robert Morris, financier and senator, advised the president to select the thirty-four year-old Hamilton, whom he described as ''damned sharp,'' Washington immediately sent his name to the Senate, where confirmation quickly followed.

With a growing family to support, and a promising law practice under way, Hamilton realized that he was endangering his personal financial security by taking the modestly compensated $3,500-per-year post. After a month on the job, he commented, ''I hazarded much, but I thought it was an occasion that called upon me to hazard.''

A gifted administrator and a fiscal genius, Hamilton had been involved in the affairs of government since 1777 when, at the age of twenty, he was appointed Washington's military aide. Five feet, seven inches tall, he maintained a strict military bearing, heightened by a touch of arrogance. A man of vast energy and deep intellect, Hamilton understood the possibilities for

Alexander Hamilton. Oil on canvas by Charles Willson Peale. Courtesy: Independence National Historical Park.

64 planned economic development under governmental direction. Above all, he preferred action to contemplation. One biographer observed that ''Hamilton's credo was audacity and yet more audacity. While others temporized, calculated the risks and paused in indecision, Hamilton acted.''

His intense ambition, his passion for order and efficiency, together with his tendency to meddle in the operations of other cabinet agencies, made him the administrative architect of the new government. The combination of special congressional powers vested in the Treasury Department, the president's relative inexperience in financial affairs, and Hamilton's expertise placed him in a stronger position than the secretaries of war and state to pursue a course of his own choosing. One member of Congress commented, ''Congress may go home. Mr. Hamilton is all-powerful and fails in nothing he attempts.''

THE STATE DEPARTMENT

Compared with Treasury, the State Department remained relatively small and restricted in the scope of its activities throughout the nation's formative years. The secretary of state conducted foreign negotiations on a highly personal basis. These relations were so delicate that no secretary considered the possibilities of delegating them to subordinates. With ministers in only five capitals—Paris, London, Lisbon, The Hague, and Madrid—there was little need for an administrative staff greater than a half-dozen clerks.

Unlike the close ties Congress set between itself and the treasury secretary, it

In 1789, George Washington named Jefferson to the post of secretary of state. Oil on canvas by Charles Willson Peale. Courtesy: Independence National Historical Park.

left the secretary of state to the president's supervision and did not even require an annual report from him. The only issue that troubled legislators in devising this statute was the president's authority to remove the secretary. This question provoked the first major crisis in relations between the legislative and executive branches under the new Constitution.

For days in June 1789, a debate raged in the House of Representatives as to whether the president should seek the Senate's advice before removing officers whose initial nominations had received Senate review. The debate focused on the right of Congress to specify conditions for the operation of an executive agency, including conditions for its chief's removal, as long as those conditions did not conflict with provisions of the Constitution. It also raised the question of whether the president would be required to share administrative authority with the Senate. On a close vote, both chambers agreed that the president could remove the officers subject to Senate confirmation without Senate concurrence.

Although President Washington was content to leave management of the nation's finances to the treasury secretary, he displayed no such detachment in the realm of foreign affairs. The president routinely consulted close associates on foreign policy matters, but did not necessarily include the secretary of state in the discussions. Jefferson expressed his frustration, on one occasion, writing that as ''Secretary of State to the United States, I can not receive any communication on the part of foreign ministers but for the purpose of laying it

before the President, and of taking his orders upon it.''

The act of July 27, 1789, which established the Department of Foreign Affairs as the first executive agency, provided only the briefest outline of its duties. They included ''Correspondence, commissions, and instructions to ministers and consuls; negotiations with public ministers from foreign states or princes; memorials or other applications from foreign ministers or other foreigners''; and ''such other matters respecting foreign affairs as the president assigned.''

Early in its existence, the State Department acquired a significant measure of responsibility for domestic, as well as foreign, affairs. Congress had specifically rejected a proposal to create a ''Home Department'' in the belief that it could achieve administrative efficiency and minimize expenses by dividing these functions among the three former Confederation agencies. The major share would go to the Foreign Affairs Department as it was less burdened with work than the Treasury and War departments. Consequently, in September 1789, the Foreign Affairs Department was renamed the Department of State and given such functions as distributing federal laws to members of Congress and the states, preparing and authenticating commissions issued by the president, conducting the decennial census, granting patents and copyrights, and safekeeping government records. The department also issued instructions to federal marshals and attorneys, and coordinated the activities of federal judges.

At its beginnings, the department included two clerks. One was in charge of the Foreign Office and the other supervised the Home Office. Housed in two rooms, this staff grew slowly with the addition of a chief clerk who carried the

title of undersecretary, a part-time interpreter, a doorkeeper, and a messenger. In 1792, Congress authorized two additional clerks. By 1800, the State Department of the United States included one secretary, one chief clerk, seven clerks, and a messenger.

When Thomas Jefferson took up his duties as secretary in March 1790, the department's entire budget, including his own $3,500 salary, amounted to $8,000. Jefferson had little to do at the outset of his term, for few foreign nations maintained active embassies at the seat of government, and the president had not yet appointed permanent ambassadors to the major European posts. At that time, a round-trip voyage to Europe required three months. With the exchange of correspondence so delayed, resident diplomats exercised a great deal of independence. In March 1791, Jefferson complained to the minister at Madrid, ''Your letter of May 6, 1789 is still the last that we have received, and that is now two years old.''

Jefferson had served as U.S. minister to France from 1785 to 1789. There he grew to appreciate that country's role in maintaining American independence of Great Britain. As secretary of state, he soon engaged in sharp political infighting with Alexander Hamilton, their mutual antagonism flaring over relations with Great Britain and France. Jefferson advocated commercial sanctions against the British to force their evacuation from posts in the Northwest. Hamilton successfully blocked this strategy, fearing a serious loss of revenue from British imports. Hostilities between the two secretaries intensified as Hamilton continued to interfere in the conduct of foreign affairs and published an anonymous series of bitter attacks on Jefferson.

When not engaged with pressing foreign business, Jefferson turned his attention and creative genius to the domestic responsibilities of his office. Among the most notable of his achievements was a lengthy and enlightening report to the House of Representatives on the topic of weights and measures. A biographer observed that his conclusions, on which the House took no action, represented ''an admirable combination of arithmetic and common sense.'' Jefferson spent a great deal of time in the administration of patents, after Congress created that system in 1790. Under the law, patent applications were to be examined by a three-man board, composed of the secretary of state, the secretary of war, and the attorney general. As a practical matter, the work fell to the secretary of state. After the attorney general ruled on the propriety of the application forms, Jefferson determined whether the individual inventions were either frivolous, unworkable, or mere modifications of existing items in common use. During his five years in office, Jefferson granted sixty-seven patents, rejecting a great many more. In 1791, weary of the task's complexity and demands on his time, Jefferson drafted a bill relieving himself of substantive responsibilities for the patent process. Two years later, Congress passed a similar measure, eliminating the examination and placing responsibility for settling disputes with the courts.

Jefferson considered these and the related duties of his office as ''hateful labors.'' As his earlier and subsequent accomplishments testified, Jefferson's greatness lay elsewhere. While secretary of state, he operated in the shadow of George Washington, who wished to be his own foreign minister. Overcome by the drudgery of the job and his battles with Hamilton, Jefferson retired at the end of 1793.

The War Department

On August 7, 1789, Congress established the War Department, and within five weeks, the Senate confirmed Henry Knox as secretary of war. The department's original staff included Knox and a clerk. A second clerk was added a few years later. By 1800, when the government moved from Philadelphia to Washington, the agency's total central and field office staff had grown to eighty. The department supervised the nation's two armories: one at Springfield, Massachusetts, and the other at Harper's Ferry, Virginia. It also included a quartermaster's section, a fortifications branch, a paymaster, an inspector general, and an Indian office.

The early record of the department was an unhappy one. Mismanagement and incompetence characterized its adminsitrative actions. A committee of the House of Representatives, investigating the late 1791 Indian defeat of General Arthur St. Clair's forces, determined that it resulted from improper organization of the expedition, lack of troop training and discipline, and ''delays consequent upon the gross and various

mismanagements and neglects in the Quartermaster's and contractor's departments.'' Alexander Hamilton moved to take matters into his own hands by requesting that his allies in the Senate push legislation giving his Treasury Department supervision of army supply services. Congress enacted Hamilton's measure in May 1792.

Henry Knox had served since 1785 as secretary of war under the Articles of Confederation. Born in Boston, Knox concluded his formal education at the age of 12. When the Revolutionary War began in 1775, he became an artillery colonel. In the war's subsequent campaigns, Knox distinguished himself as a military commander and became a favorite of General Washington. Still, Knox proved to be a clumsy civilian administrator, undercut by a president who considered military affairs his own greatest strength. Plagued by the pressure of gambling debts, Knox became preoccupied with land speculation schemes designed to restore his family's financial health. These ventures led to further indebtedness and numberous law suits. Knox resigned as war secretary in 1794.

The Post Office

In 1789, the nation's mail system consisted of seventy-five post offices and 1,875 miles of post roads, running principally from Boston, Massachusetts, to Petersburg, Virginia. In September of that year, Congress passed legislation temporarily continuing post office operations as they had existed under the Articles of Confederation. Members demonstrated no interest in creating a

Henry Knox's military experience made him George Washington's choice for secretary of war in the first Cabinet. Oil on panel by Gilbert Stuart. Courtesy: Museum of Fine Arts, Boston.

separate postal department, or of merging its functions with an existing department. The statute simply provided that "the Postmaster General shall be subject to the direction of the President of the United States."

In the years before 1789, the Confederation Congress viewed the post office as a vital source of governmental revenue. In 1790, the office produced a $5,000 profit on income of $38,000. In 1792, Congress specifically placed the post office within the jurisdiction of Hamilton's Treasury Department, in recognition of its revenue-producing functions. This provoked a protest from Secretary of State Jefferson, who feared that "the department of the Treasury possessed already such an influence as to swallow up the whole executive powers, and that future presidents (not supported by the weight of character which [Washington] possessed) would not be able to make head against this department."

By 1796, the department's profit-producing incentive yielded to another essential function—its capacity for communicating governmental actions to all sections of the nation. As Washington advised the House of Representatives in 1792, "The circulation of political intelligence through these vehicles is justly reckoned among the surest means of preventing the degeneracy of a free government, as well as recommending every salutary public measure to the confidence and cooperation of all virtuous citizens."

In 1790, the post office consisted of Postmaster General Samuel Osgood, who earned $1,500—less than half the annual salary rate of the department secretaries—an assistant, and a clerk. His principal duties were to designate post offices, to select and maintain contact with deputy postmasters, to award contracts for carrying mail, and to keep accounts. The actual work of moving the mail fell to the deputy postmasters and contractors, whose salaries were paid by local postal revenues. Retention of competent deputy postmasters proved to be the postmaster general's greatest headache. Those part-time positions held few attractions, except in major cities. Osgood resigned in 1791 rather than move with the rest of the government from New York to Philadelphia. The post office remained a subordinate agency until 1825 when it achieved independent status as a result of presidential wishes to control politically attractive deputy postmaster appointments.

The Attorney General

Like the postmaster general, the attorney general served as a second-level presidential appointee during the federal government's early years. President Washington viewed Attorney General Edmund Randolph, who held that post from 1790-1794, simply as his legal advisor. Under provisions of the 1789 Judiciary Act, which established his position, Randolph was to prosecute all suits in the Supreme Court that involved the interest of the United States government. That statute also directed him to provide legal advice to the president and department heads when they requested it. At the outset, as there were no cases before the Supreme Court, and as the president seldom sought his advice, Randolph had virtually nothing to do. Reflecting this status, the attorney general received less than half the salary of cabinet secretaries and had no government staff. He was expected to conduct official business from his personal law office and to maintain a private legal practice when he was not advising the president or other federal officials. On matters of major legal consequence, President Washington frequently bypassed his attorney general in favor of Hamilton and Jefferson. The secretary of state retained responsibility for supervising federal district attorneys. Despite his persistent efforts, Randolph was unable to acquire law enforcement responsibilities. He left the position in 1794 to replace Jefferson as secretary of state.

Conclusion

Washington, Hamilton, Jefferson, and Knox, along with Osgood and Randolph, by and large built successfully on the executive structure established under the Articles of Confederation and by Congress under the Constitution. These leaders of the early executive departments achieved much for the government in a nation that less than a generation earlier had suffered the dependence of colonial rule. In these formative years, the executive agencies established a high level of legitimacy and moral integrity, as well as a degree of autonomy from close legislative direction. The president clearly exercised substantial administration authority and responsibility for conduct of the new government's official business. He effectively delegated authority to department heads and through them to their immediate subordinates and field representatives, while retaining controls over their performance. Despite Hamilton's occasional intrusions into operations of other departments, executive agency leaders formed relatively stable relationships based on precedent, law, and presidential directives. To be sure, the achievements of these men were not untouched by failure. The Post Office was slow and unreliable. The Treasury and War departments remained unable to devise an efficient system for procuring army supplies. The patent system, after a period of rigorous executive involvement, was abandoned to the courts. Despite these shortcomings, the occasion for celebrating the Constitution's two hundredth anniversary is due, in great measure, to the successful establishment of the early executive departments.

*Reprinted, with permission, from *this Constitution*, No. 17, Winter 1987. Washington, D.C.: Project '87.

FOR FURTHER READING

Marcus Cunliffe, *The American Heritage History of the Presidency*. New York: American Heritage Publishing Co., 1968.

Ralph Ketcham, *Presidents Above Party: The First American Presidency*. Chapel Hill, N.C.: University of North Carolina Press, 1984.

Forrest McDonald, *Alexander Hamilton: A Biography*. Boston: Little Brown & Co., 1979.

Dumas Malone, *Jefferson and the Rights of Man*. New York: W.W. Norton Company, 1979.

Leonard D. White, *The Federalists: A Study in Administrative History*. New York: The Macmillan Company, 1948.

"Very busy and not a little anxious:"

ALEXANDER HAMILTON, AMERICA'S FIRST SECRETARY OF THE TREASURY

by Joanne B. Freeman

George Washington wrote: ''that he is ambitious I shall readily grant, but it is of the laudable kind which prompts a man to excel in whatever he takes in hand.''[1] Thomas Jefferson called him ''a colossus to the anti-republican party. Without numbers, he is a host within himself.''[2] Senator William Maclay grumbled that he ''is all-powerful and fails in nothing he attempts.''[3] These men were speaking of Alexander Hamilton, America's first secretary of the treasury. Hamilton had experienced a meteoric rise from obscurity to power, prestige, and public office. By the age of thirty-four, he was the head of America's most active and influential executive department, the Treasury, and his actions as secretary were a driving force behind the fledgling nation's development.

Hamilton's rise was all the more remarkable when viewed in the light of his origins. His youth was marked by poverty, hardship, and turmoil. Born in 1755 on the Caribbean island of Nevis, Hamilton was the illegitimate son of James Hamilton, a ne'er-do-well Scottish merchant, and Rachel Faucett, the descendant of French immigrants to the island. By the age of thirteen, he was orphaned witout any inheritance and forced to fend for himself. Within a few years, however, his precocity had brought him into the public eye, and friends raised money to send the boy to America to receive a formal education. In 1773, Hamilton entered King's College (now Columbia University), but never completed his studies. The Revolutionary War was in its formative stages, and swept away by his passionate ideals and his longing for glory,

This portrait of Alexander Hamilton was painted by John Trumbull in 1792 at the request of the New York City Chamber of Commerce to honor the treasury secretary's achievements. Oil on canvas. Courtesy: Donaldson, Lufkin and Jenrette Americana Collection.

Hamilton was soon serving in the Continental Army. By 1777, he had been brought to the attention of General Washington, who appointed him aide-de-camp. He worked diligently by Washington's side throughout most of the remainder of the war (despite occasional personal disagreements), and led troops bravely during the Battle of Yorktown in 1781. His service as an aide influenced him greatly in later years, for not only did he establish himself as a gifted assistant to George Washington, but he saw firsthand the weaknesses of the Articles of Confederation.

After the war, Hamilton won admission to the New York Bar after only months of intensive study, and established a law practice in New York City. In 1782, unsatisfied with the weak government inherent in the country's recent Articles of Confederation, he urged the New York legislature to pass a resolution for a general convention of the states to amend the Articles. This was the first formal step of a campaign that he had begun in 1780 to strengthen the government of the United States.[4] He served as a New York delegate to the Annapolis Convention in 1786, and drafted that body's report calling for a new convention to strengthen the powers of the federal government.

In 1787, Hamilton served as a New York delegate to the Federal Convention in Philadelphia. However, his effectiveness as an advocate of a strong national government was limited by the opposition of the other two delegates from New York (who soon left the Convention altogether), and by the uncompromising nationalism of his own proposed constitutional design. In the end, Hamilton signed the proposed Constitution, although unauthorized to do so by the State of New York.

At this point, Hamilton's passionate belief in the necessity of adopting the new Costitution led him to join forces with James Madison and John Jay in composing *The Federalist*. This series of eighty-five newspaper essays was designed to explain and defend the newly created Constitution, and to rally support for its ratification. Hamilton wrote fifty-one of the essays, sometimes with the printer waiting at his side for him to finish. Today, *The Federalist* is considered one of the most important works in American political science.

Hamilton and Jay also joined forces to lead the outnumbered Federalists of New York against the Constitution's opponents, the Antifederalists, led by Hamilton's former convention colleagues, Robert Yates and John Lansing, Jr., along with Melancton Smith and the powerful Governor George Clinton. After an intense struggle, the New York ratifying convention in Poughkeepsie finally voted to adopt the Constitution on July 26, 1788. Three days earlier, the Federalists of New York City had celebrated the ratification of the Consitution by ten states—and put pressure on the Poughkeepsie convention—by holding a parade, complete with a model ship named the "Hamilton," featuring the figure of Hamilton holding the Constitution.

Once the Constitution had been ratified by a majority of states, the new national government had to be put into effect. George Washington was unanimously elected to serve as the first president, but his Cabinet nominations were still to come. For secretary of the treasury, several people suggested Hamilton, and these recommendations, combined with Washington's personal knowledge of Hamilton's gifts, led to his official appointment as treasury secretary on September 11, 1789.

One of Hamilton's contemporaries described him at about this time as "middle size, thin in person, but remarkably erect and dignified in his deportment. His hair was turned back from his forehead, powdered and collected in a club behind. His complexion was exceedingly fair, and varying from this only by the almost feminine rosiness of his cheeks. His might be considered as to figure and color, and uncommonly handsome face. When at rest, it had rather a severe, thoughtful expression, but when engaged in conversation it easily assumed an attractive smile."[5] Boyishly handsome, dignified in his manner, always dressed in the height of fashion, Hamilton cut a striking figure in the surroundings of the new federal government.

The treasury secretary's task was not an easy one. The Treasury Department was the largest and most active of Washington's cabinet; it included more than thirty employees. In contrast, the Department of State employed only six men, and the War Department only three. Because of the Treasury Department's importance, Congress was very cautious with its implemenation. They realized that the authority given to the treasury department was far-reaching, and they feared what one man would do with this power. Originally, Congress even considered appointing a three-member treasury board as a protective measure, as they had after the controversial Robert Morris stepped down as superintendent of finance in 1784. In the end, though they did gamble on creating the post of treasury secretary, they built many safeguards into the office.

Hamilton knew that his new job posed grave risks. In every western nation, the post of minister of finance had been a "graveyard of reputations... from which no man returned with his name unsmirched."[6] After accepting his new position, he wrote that "In undertaking the task I hazarded much, but I thought it an occasion that called upon me to hazard."[7] Taking great pains in his public and private conduct to avoid accusations of graft, Hamilton not only sold all of the securities owed him by the government, but declined to collect the benefits due him as a war veteran and gave up his law practice entirely. With these actions, Hamilton committed himself to supporting a growing family of five on the treasury secretary's salary alone—a mere $3,000 a year. No caution, however, was too great at the outset, for as Hamilton recognized, "...to every man concerned in the administration of the finances of a Country....Suspicion is ever eagle eyed, and the most innocent things are apt to be misinterpreted."[8]

Hamilton would have to be more than cautious to untangle the nation's chaotic finances. The task before him was enormous. The new federal government had inherited a mass of debts, mostly foreign loans with payment due and government securities payable

This cylinder desk was used by Alexander Hamilton during his term as secretary of the treasury. Courtesy: Museum of the City of New York.

Drawn & Engraved by W. Birch & Son.

Published by R. Campbell & Co. No. 30 Chesnut Street Philad.ª 1798.

BANK OF THE UNITED STATES, With a View of Third Street PHILADELPHIA.

originally to war veterans who were owed wartime salaries. The states' debts posed, if anything, an even greater threat to the American economy. Some states had already tried to pay some of their debts, others had not. To complicate matters futher, each of the thirteen states had different currencies with different values, and few accurate records existed regarding any previous financial dealings. The new republic was beginning life with a total debt of more than fifty million dollars.

In addition, Hamilton recognized, as did others, that the rest of the world was closely watching the American experience in government. Respectability and stability were essential prerequisites for the United States before it could take a place of honor on the international stage. As secretary of the treasury, Hamilton was trusted with the task of establishing financial stability and system in his department, in his country, and in American dealings with the world at large.

Hamilton approached the challenge before him with a coherent but controversial ideology intended to shape the nation's economic, social, and political life. For years, he had railed against the weakness of the Confederation Congress, deploring its ''want of method and energy.''[9] His vision for the future of America consisted of an ''energetic'' national government, working to foster industry among the nation's inhabitants and insuring financial stability domestically and abroad. In an age of loosely linked states, each jealously guarding its independence and interests, Hamilton was one of the first and foremost theorists of American nationalism; as an immigrant to the colonies, his freedom

from any state's ties allowed him the perspective of seeing things on a broader, national scale. In a country just freed from what was felt to be a despotic monarchy, Hamilton dared to preach the need for a strong government with an equally strong executive at its head. Although America at this time was largely agrarian, Hamilton was one of the primary supporters of industrial growth; that the ''cultivation of the earth,'' he said, has ''a title to anything like an exclusive predilection, in any country, ought to be admitted with great caution.''[10] And, perhaps most controversially, Hamilton continually stressed the need for attracting the wealthy and powerful to support the national government. His nationalist, centralizing policies outraged many in the 1790s.

The uncertainties surrounding America's new, untried government combined to provide a perfect arena for a man such as Hamilton to display his talents. While the ill-defined nature of the new federal government induced hesitancy in many, it spurred Hamilton to action, enabling him to use his administrative genius to develop policies and systems that would implement his nationalist vision.

Those who did not share his vision faced fierce opposition, for Hamilton was never meek where his heartfelt beliefs and ambitions were concerned. Convinced of his qualifications and eager for the ''opportunity of doing good,''[11] he never hesitated in stepping

forward to act as he saw fit. Although he always felt that he was acting in the country's best interest, he often provoked anger and outrage when perceived as overstepping his bounds. Aggressive, ambitious, audacious, opinionated, and seemingly tireless in working toward his goals, he never failed to arouse opposition. Indeed, as Hamilton's policies developed, his views and forceful backing of them led to the organization of groups for or against him, eventually resulting in the rise of political parties in American politics.

Hamilton had his first real impact as secretary of the treasury almost immediately in the fall of 1789. Creditors had petitioned the government for payment of portions of their debt, and Congress passed the problem to Hamilton with great relief, asking him for a report on public credit. This report, his first attempt to articulate his economic and political policies, was of the utmost importance. As Hamilton wrote to a friend, ''you may imagine that... I am very busy and not a little anxious.''[12] On January 14, 1790, Hamilton delivered his *Report Relative to a Provision for the Support of Public Credit* to Congress. Its impact was explosive.

Hamilton's *Report* proposed to recalculate the foreign debt and convert it into a fund, with an obligation to use a set portion of the yearly national revenue toward its repayment. This was aimed at establishing America's credit abroad. Second, the national government would assume responsibility for all the states' debts. This policy would tie creditors to the national government instead of to state governments, remove the need for states to compete with the national government in taxation, and start all of the states out on an equal fiscal footing. Third, regarding the government's notes of debt to war

This building housed the Bank of the United States in Philadelphia. Courtesy: New York Public Library Prints Division, Stokes Collection.

veterans, Hamilton proposed to pay off the value of all securities in full to their present holders; he rejected discrimination either in favor of the veterans who originally held them, or against the speculators who had bought them at a fraction of their face value from veterans desperate for cash.

As a veteran, Hamilton surely felt the unfairness of this aspect of his financial plan. As a finanical administrator, a lawyer, and a nationalist, he realized that these securities were written contracts, committing the government to redeeming them at face value to the present owner. If the government began toying with the value of the certificates, or negating fair transactions between buyers and sellers, its credit would be destroyed. In addition, if the securities' value was changed, they could no longer be used as a form of negotiable currency. Finally, it would be impossible to retrace each certificate's path of ownership; there were few accurate records to follow, and the government could not afford to pay every person who had ever held a security.

The *Report* threw Congress into an uproar. States with discharged or partly paid debts felt cheated, and opposed being taxed to help pay other states' debts. Jealous of their individual rights and interests, few states' representatives thought on a national scale. Hamilton's policies would also be highly profitable to wealthy speculators, frequently at the expense of poverty-stricken war widows and veterans. As news of Hamilton's proposals spread, this situation worsened, for speculators began to race through the countryside, frantically buying up veterans' notes in the hope of increasing their profit. Hamilton was soon depicted as a friend to the wealthy and powerful, at the expense of the "common man."

The assumption of state debts proved to be the sticking point for Hamilton's proposal. As debate continued for months, the secretary grew increasingly despairing. If the bill was defeated, he foresaw inestimable damage to the national government, loss of America's credit both at home and abroad, and the possible failure of the entire constitutional system of government. One day in July of 1790, Secretary of State Thomas Jefferson encountered Hamilton pacing before the president's house. Jefferson noticed that Hamilton's appearance was not typically spruce; he looked "sombre, haggard & dejected beyond description, even his dress uncouth & neglected"[13]—in short, like a man under great stress. Hamilton pleaded with Jefferson to urge some of his friends in Congress to switch their votes in favor of assumption. Without Jefferson's help, Hamilton declared, he feared for the Union's survival. The two planned to meet the next day at Jefferson's house for dinner, and there, a compromise was reached. Jefferson mediated between Hamilton and Representative James Madison of Virginia, the leading opponent of assumption. Madison agreed to cease active opposition to assumption, and Hamilton, in turn, agreed to support the moving of the nation's capital to Philadelphia for ten years, and finally to a site on the banks of the Potomac. Hamilton also agreed to rework the assumption formulas to ensure more favorable treatment for Virginia. This compromise, along with dealings between several other influential political leaders, led to congressional acceptance of national assumption of state debts.

This early collaboration between Jefferson and Hamilton is remarkable when viewed in the light of their eventual bitter political enmity. Later, as Hamilton's foremost antagonist, Jefferson regretted his part in the compromise, even claiming that Hamilton had tricked him into cooperating. The two men's political ideologies were so directly opposed that their eventual clash was inevitable. Hamilton's view of the nation as an industrial power, governed by a strong national government and a powerful executive, and supported by attracting the interest of the wealthy and powerful, was diametrically opposed to Jefferson's vision of a simple agrarian nation, united under a far weaker federal government. As Hamilton pressed his proposals through Congress and within the Cabinet, lobbying, persuading, and writing to achieve his goals, he increasingly felt resistance from Jefferson.

This resistance was aggravated by Hamilton's frequent forays into the affairs of other departments. Admittedly, administrative boundaries were less sharply defined than they are today, and President Washington frequently asked all of his Cabinet members for opinions on matters relating to specific departments. Hamilton's passionate beliefs, however, led him to propound his views on foreign affairs in as vigorously ag-

This shield-back chair is typical of New York furniture of the Federal period. One of a large set originally owned by Elizabeth and Alexander Hamilton, this chair was used at ''The Grange,'' their New York City home. Courtesy: New York State Museum, Albany. Gift of Wunsch Americana Foundation.

gessive a manner as he did his economic policies. His influence in affairs of state, combined with his eventual inheritance of the position of acting secretary of war after Henry Knox retired, made Hamilton more of a prime minister than a treasury secretary. Jefferson increasingly grew to resent and fear the range of Hamilton's influence and power, and gradually emerged as the leader of the anti-Hamilton forces. Hamilton, in turn, saw Jefferson's attacks as a form of personal animosity. Unable to understand how Jefferson could be blind to the future greatness of America as he envisioned it, Hamilton interpreted Jefferson's actions as motivated by malice and ambition, aimed at working against the national government. Their rivalry grew so heated that President Washington was soon forced to demand a written promise of compromise from each man.

The rivalry between the two Cabinet members spread into print, and two newspapers emerged as its principal vehicles. *The Gazette of the United States* was Federalist, as Hamilton's supporters were now called, and the *Republican National Gazette* supported Jefferson. Both papers were full of condemnatory accusations, and both Hamilton and Jefferson suffered from the onslaught of abuse. Hamilton, however, was always hypersensitive concerning issues of personal honor, and always inclined to fight every fight himself. He began to write extensively both to defend his integrity and to reveal to the public the dangers and malice he saw in his opponent. Jefferson, more wisely, chose to allow others to fight his fights. Unfortunately for Hamilton, his efforts also targeted him

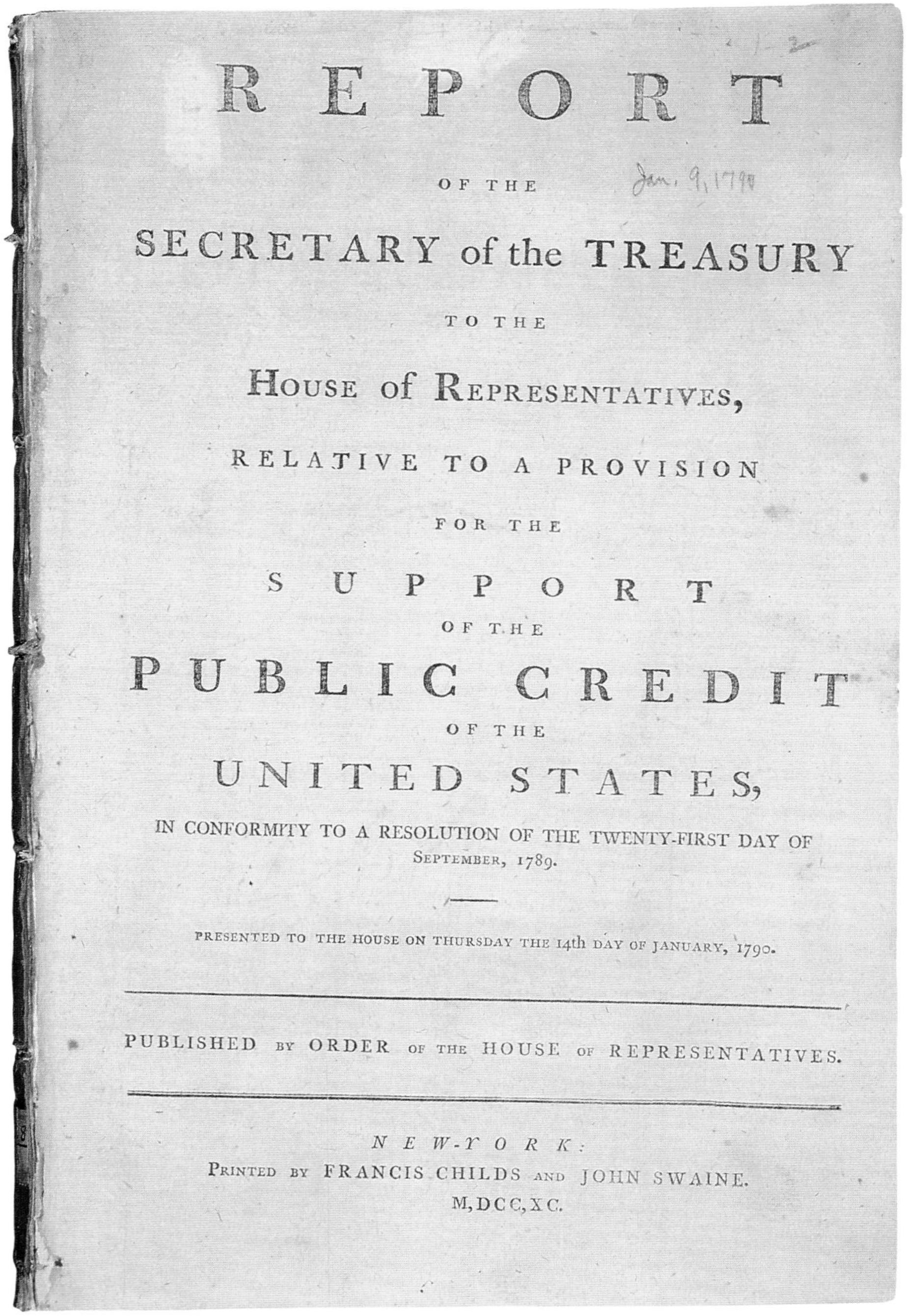

REPORT

OF THE

SECRETARY of the TREASURY

Jan. 9, 1790

TO THE

House of Representatives,

RELATIVE TO A PROVISION

FOR THE

SUPPORT

OF THE

PUBLIC CREDIT

OF THE

UNITED STATES,

IN CONFORMITY TO A RESOLUTION OF THE TWENTY-FIRST DAY OF
SEPTEMBER, 1789.

PRESENTED TO THE HOUSE ON THURSDAY THE 14th DAY OF JANUARY, 1790.

PUBLISHED BY ORDER OF THE HOUSE OF REPRESENTATIVES.

NEW-YORK:
PRINTED BY FRANCIS CHILDS AND JOHN SWAINE.
M,DCC,XC.

as the man to defeat to overcome the Federalist party, and promoted Jefferson as the head of the opposition and the defender of the "common man." Representative John Nicholas of Virginia summed up the prevalent Republican view of Hamilton when he asked Washington, "Did it never occur to you that the divisions of America might be ended by the sacrafice [sic] of this one man?"[14]

Despite increased opposition, Hamilton continued to push his policies through Congress. One of his key proposals, set forth in his *Report on a National Bank*, was passed by Congress, but when President Washington received the bill for his approval, he asked for the opinions of his Cabinet members. Both Jefferson and Attorney General Edmund Randolph declared it unconstitutional—nowhere in the Constitution was the power to institute a bank granted to the government. Requesting that Madison prepare a veto message, Washington also asked Hamilton to defend his plan. The treasury secretary's response established the policy of "broad" construction of the Constitution. Hamilton declared that the government could act in ways not explicitly authorized by the Constitution, as long as the proposed actions were not specifically barred by the Constitution and were in pursuit of goals contained within the Constitution. This interpretation gave the government increased flexibility and power, in accordance with Hamilton's views. Washington accepted Hamilton's views and signed the bank bill into law. More important, Hamilton's views became key principles of our constitutional system. Indeed, President Jefferson himself resorted to broad construction of the Constitution

Title page of Alexander Hamilton's Report on the Public Credit, *1790. Courtesy: Library of Congress.*

to support his acquisition of the Louisiana Territory in 1803.

Hamilton's faults as a political leader were many. Anxious to accomplish what he set out to achieve, he frequently tried too hard, said too much, pushed too far, and alienated too many. Fiercely convinced of the accuracy and necessity of his ideas, he was usually unwilling to compromise, sometimes to the point of committing gross errors of judgment. His constant sensitivity to his honor and status as a gentleman at times made him seem arrogant and vain. And although a brilliant orator and spokesperson for his policies, he was rarely successful at appealing to the public at large.

Yet despite his shortcomings, Hamilton was a man of strong actions and strong words at a time when strength was needed. And because his heartfelt vision of America's future proved more prophetic than his opponents' views, his unremitting campaign for a strong national government may well be his most valuable legacy to posterity. In 1789, our new national government was untried, untested, and unproven. Lines were not yet drawn. Processes were not yet established. America had almost no sense of itself as a nation. Hamilton's bold policies for financial stability led to a sense of national pride and a national identity. His aggressiveness and ambitions for national power led to far more. As a young soldier, Hamilton had jotted down a brief extract from Demosthenes in his pay book: ''As a general marches at the head of his troops, so ought wise politicians, if I dare use the expression, to march at the head of affairs; insomuch that they ought not to wait the event, to know what measures to take; but the measures which they have taken, ought to produce the *event*.'' [15] This sentiment seemed to be Hamilton's guiding principle as treasury secretary. His bold actions, often ignor-

ing departmental boundaries, forced Congress to define those boundaries and the workings of the new national government. Furthermore, Hamilton's aggressive tactics hastened the adoption of principles of constitutional interpretations that have shaped our national development for nearly two centuries.

[1] Allan McLane Hamilton, *The Intimate Life of Alexander Hamilton* (New York: Charles Scribner's Sons, 1911), 53.

[2] Forrest McDonald, *Alexander Hamilton, A Biography* (New York: W.W. Norton & Company, 1979), 316.

[3] Claude G. Bowers, *Jefferson and Hamilton, The Struggle for Democracy in America* (Boston: Houghton Mifflin Company, 1925), p.74.

[4] Harold C. Syrett, ed., *The Papers of Alexander Hamilton*, 26 vols. (New York: Columbia University Press, 1961-79), 400.

[5] William Sullivan, *The Public Men of the Revolution* (Philadelphia: Carey & Hart, 1847), 260.

[6] John C. Miller, *Alexander Hamilton, Portrait in Paradox* (New York: Harper & Brothers, Publishers, 1959), 225.

[7] *Ibid.*, 226.

[8] Syrett, ed., *The papers of Alexander Hamilton*, 6:1.

[9] *Ibid.*, 2:404.

[10] Richard B. Morris, ed., *Alexander hamilton and the Founding of the Nation* (New York: The Dial Press, 1957), 361.

[11] *Ibid.*, 572.

[12] Robert A. Hendrickson, *The Rise and Fall of Alexander Hamilton* (New York: Dodd, Mead & Company, 1981), 260.

[13] Miller, *Alexander Hamilton, Portrait in Paradox*, 250.

[14] McDonald, *Alexander Hamilton, A Biography*, 291.

[15] E.P. Panagopoulos, ed., *Alexander Hamilton's Pay Book* (Detroit, MI: Wayne State University Press, 1961), 45.

Morton J. Frisch, ed., *Selected Writings and Speeches of Alexander Hamilton.* Washington, D.C.: American Enterprise Institute for Public Policy Research, 1985.

Forrest McDonald, *Alexander Hamilton, A Biography.* New York: W.W. Norton & Company, 1979.

John C. Miller, *Alexander-Hamilton, Portrait in Paradox.* New York: Harper & Row, Publishers, 1959.

_____, *The Federalist Era.* New York: Harper & Row, Publishers, 1960.

Broadus Mitchell, *Alexander Hamilton.* 2 vols. New York: The Macmillan Company, 1957.

_____, *Alexander Hamilton, A Concise Biography.* New York: Oxford University Press, 1976.

Richard B. Morris, ed., *Alexander Hamilton and the Founding of the Nation.* New York: The Dial Press, 1957.

The Birth of the Federal Court System

by David Eisenberg, Christine R. Jordan,
Maeva Marcus, and Emily F. Van Tassel

As the first justices of the Supreme Court were preparing to undertake their duties, President Washington wrote to them expressing his feelings about the importance of the job they were about to begin. ''I have always been persuaded that the stability and success of the National Government, and consequently the happiness of the People of the United States, would depend, in a considerable degree, on the Interpretation and Execution of its Laws,'' Washington observed. ''In my opinion, therefore, it is important that the Judiciary System should not only be independent in its operations, but as perfect as possible in its formation.''

THE UNITED STATES CONSTITUTION ARTICLE III

The Founders of the new nation believed that the establishment of a national judiciary was one of their most important tasks. Yet Article III of the Constitution of the United States, the provision that deals with the judicial branch of government, is markedly shorter than Articles I and II which created the legislative and executive branches. Moreover, at the Constitutional Convention, the delegates spent relatively little time discussing judicial power. Instead, they left the resolution of those issues on which they could not easily agree to the Congress that would come into being after the new frame of government was approved. Thus, the story of the development of the judicial power under the Constitution concerns much more than an understanding of the text of Article III.

The Constitution had not sprung full blown from the crucible of revolution but instead resulted from a growing recognition throughout the states that

The Seal of the United States Supreme Court. Courtesy: The Supreme Court Historical Society.

the Confederation was inadequate and that a stronger national government was needed if the United States was to survive. The lack of an independent judiciary to decide controversies of a national and international nature contributed to the Confederation's weakness. Congress had set up the very limited Court of Appeals in Cases of Capture to hear disputes involving ships seized during the Revolution, but it did not meet regularly and had no power to enforce its decrees.

Thus, the concept of a national judiciary was a new one in the late 1780s and its embodiment in Article III a cause of much concern. The structure of the judiciary was a rock upon which the Constitution could founder when it went before the states for ratification; hence, Federalist efforts had focused on creating a constitutional framework that would give wide latitude to Congress to flesh out the particulars of a court system. By creating a structure that left all the details of form and content to congressional discretion, Federalists hoped to allay—or at least postpone until after the Constitution was safely ratified—Antifederalist fears that the national judiciary would swallow up the state courts.

Article III of the Constitution created a federal "judicial Power" but defined it in only the broadest of terms. Section 1 provided that power "shall be vested in one supreme Court, and in such inferior Courts as the Congress may, from time to time, ordain and establish." Section 2 specified the types of cases to which the federal judicial power extended, giving the Supreme Court original jurisdiction to hear "all Cases affecting Ambassadors, other public Ministers and Consuls, and those in which a State shall be a Party." In all other categories enumerated in the section, cases would originate in lower courts but could be brought to the Supreme Court on appeal, subject to "such exceptions, and under such Regulations as the Congress shall make." Hence, the Constitution left to congressional discretion the content and extent of the appellate jurisdiction of the Supreme Court, and by implication, the entire jurisdiction of any lower federal courts that might be established.

The text of Article III set down certain basic principles, but the debates during the ratification process indicated that in many states there was dissatisfaction with the broad language of the judicial article and a strong demand for some additional constitutional safeguards. In his *Federalist* No. 78, Alexander Hamilton downplayed the importance of the federal judiciary by denominating it the "least dangerous" of the three branches; in No. 80 he reminded his readers that any inconvenience suggested by the generality of the plan should not condemn it, as

the national legislature will have ample authority to make such exceptions, and to prescribe such regulations as will be calculated to obviate or remove these inconveniences. The possibility of particular mischiefs can never be viewed, by a well-informed mind, as a solid objection to a general principle, which is calculated to avoid general mischiefs and to obtain general advantages.

Ideas as to what those inconveniences might be, and how best to deal with them, began to circulate well before any lawmaker had so much as dipped his quill into the inkwell. Soon after the Constitutional Convention adjourned in September 1787, people were expressing fears that an extensive federal court system would prove too expensive, drag hapless defendants hundreds of miles from home, and undermine state sovereignty and individual liberties.

Antifederalist forces led by two Virginians—George Mason, who had refused to sign the Constitution, and Richard Henry Lee, who had refused to attend the Constitutional Convention—began an immediate campaign in the press and in the state ratifying conventions to have the federal judicial power amended before ratification of the Constitution. Recalling the harsh treatment meted out by colonial governors and British vice-admiralty judges in the years prior to the Revolution, Antifederalists were particulary concerned with protecting the rights of the criminally accused. They called for a bill of rights to include protection of the right to a grand jury indictment, to a speedy and public trial by an impartial jury drawn from the vicinage (i.e., vicinity in which the crime was committed), to know the cause and nature of accusations, to confront witnesses and compel them to appear in court, to assistance of counsel, to due process of law, and to protection against self-incrimination, double jeopardy, excessive bail, fines, and cruel and unusual punishment. In non-criminal cases, Antifederalists also wanted as much jury protection for the individual as possible: jury trials in all civil cases, protection for jury verdicts by limiting appellate courts' power to review juries' factual determinations, and the right to due process under the law.

In addition to a written guarantee of individual rights, Antifederalists favored a number of explicit proposals to limit the power of the federal courts. At least half the state ratifying conventions recommended limiting or abol-

John Jay, first chief justice of the United States Supreme Court. Portrait, 1786, by Joseph Wright. Courtesy: The New-York Historical Society.

ishing diversity jurisdiction—a jurisdiction based solely on the fact that the parties are citizens of different states. A proposal to restrict appeals to the Supreme Court to cases involving only large sums of money also gained considerable support during the ratification process of 1787-1788. Another Antifederalist proposal, which came to have support among some cost-conscious Federalists as well, was the use of state courts as lower federal courts. Roger Sherman of Connecticut, a member of the Constitutional Convention and soon to be a member of the First Congress, endorsed just such an idea in his essay "A Citizen of New Haven," published on January 1, 1787. Even such a leading Federalist as James Madison, on the eve of his election to the House of Representatives in January 1789, acknowledged the need for some sort of bill of rights to protect individual liberties and some sort of restriction on appeals in the federal courts. As early as March 15, 1789, the staunch Massachusetts Federalist Fisher Ames, reported from New York to a friend in New England that a judicial plan was being discussed by three or four persons that would limit diversity suits and suits involving foreigners to cases where the sum in controversy was over five hundred dollars. He further commented that the great objectives of low cost and allaying state-federal jealousies might best be accomplished by narrowing rather than expanding federal jurisdiction.

THE JUDICIARY ACT OF 1789

It fell to the First Federal Congress to interpret the various sections of Article III and to take into consideration the amendments demanded by several states as the price of ratification. By drawing up the Bill of Rights and enacting the Judiciary Act of 1789, the

84 First Congress met the concerns of many. It was able to establish a working judicial system that pleased no one completely, but which could be changed as experience showed it to be necessary or desirable.

While the House of Representatives began its work on the first important piece of financial legislation, a revenue system, the Senate, acknowledging the pivotal role that the federal court system must play in the new government, began its legislative work by appointing a committee to prepare a judiciary bill. The committee as formed on April 7, 1789, consisted of one senator from each state: Oliver Ellsworth of Connecticut, William Paterson of New Jersey, Caleb Strong of Massachusetts, Richard Henry Lee of Virginia, Richard Bassett of Delaware, William Maclay of Pennsylvania, William Few of Georgia, and Paine Wingate of New Hampshire. Charles Carroll of Maryland and Ralph Izard of South Carolina, arriving late for the opening of Congress, were added to the roster six days later.

Only Ellsworth, Paterson, and Strong of the ten committee members on whom the judiciary's fate depended, could claim any sizable technical legal expertise; but most had a strong political and legislative background. Six had been members of the Continental Congress (Ellsworth, Few, Carroll, Izard, Wingate, and Lee). Five had been members of the Constitutional Convention (Ellsworth, Strong, Paterson, Bassett, and Few). Five had been members of their state ratifying convention (Ellsworth, Strong, Few, Bassett, and Izard). Nearly all had held a variety of state offices. Politically all were Federalists with the exception of Richard Henry Lee, a leading Antifederalist and a harsh critic of an expansive federal judiciary, and William Maclay, who was elected by Pennsylvania to repre-

sent the state's agricultural interests.

The combination of extensive legal experience and firsthand knowledge of the Constitution seems to have been a key factor in determining who would write the bill; for it was the three men with both characteristics—Ellsworth, Paterson, and Strong—in whose handwriting the first draft appeared. Ellsworth, in particular, dominated the proceedings, from the first page of handwritten text, through the debates, to the final conference with the House. "This vile bill is a child of his" fumed the irascible diarist, William Maclay, "and he defends it with the care of a parent, even in wrath and anger." Maclay's disgruntlement aside, Ellsworth was eminently qualified for the job of creating a bill that, after all the politics were exhausted, still had perforce to deal with a multitude of arcane details. Ellsworth's background included service on the Continental Congress Committee on Appeals (giving him firsthand experience with the problems of appellate jurisdiction in a federal system); he had also been a member of the Governor's Council and a state court judge in Connecticut, as well as a member of the Constitutional Convention and the Connecticut ratifying convention. Caleb Strong had served in the Constitutional Convention and the Massachusetts ratifying convention. William Paterson had been attorney general of New Jersey and had also been present at Philadelphia for the drafting of the Constitution.

Within three weeks, the committee had drafted a set of guiding principles

that clearly reflected the concerns raised during the ratification debate over limiting federal court jurisdiction. The resolutions indicated that the committee favored a small judiciary and had already adopted the idea of limiting non-criminal cases tried in federal courts to those involving large sums of money. The structure created by the committee included a Supreme Court and two levels of lower federal courts. The draft bill specified a six-judge Supreme Court, to convene twice yearly in the national capital. During the months when they were not sitting as the Supreme Court, the justices were made responsible for hearing trials and appeals on circuit in the several states, sitting in pairs in conjunction with a district court judge. The district court judges would come from the courts established in each state as federal trial courts, responsible primarily for hearing admiralty cases. The circuit court's jurisdiction in non-criminal cases was restricted in most instances to cases of at least three hundred dollars or more. Appeals to the Supreme Court could only be made in cases involving amounts above two thousand dollars. Finally, the committee gave the Supreme Court explicit powers of judicial review over state supreme court decisions involving federal law. There seemed to have been a consensus that only cases involving substantial amounts of money should be subject to federal appellate review unless an interpretation of the federal Constitution, a statute, or a treaty were in question.

The drafting efforts of Paterson, Ellsworth, and Strong culminated in a first reading before the full Senate on June 12. When printed for distribution

and Senate debate, the bill ran sixteen pages. District court jurisdiction, which was to give rise to the greatest debate in both houses, had been fleshed out in more detail. In addition to exclusive original jurisdiction over all civil admiralty and maritime cases, district courts were also given jurisdiction over some other lesser federal matters. The committee made trial by jury protections explicit in several situations, among them criminal cases and suits brought by the United States for amounts over one hundred dollars. Similarly, jury trials were required in civil and criminal cases in the circuit courts and in original Supreme Court cases involving individuals who were United States citizens. It is clear that Richard Henry Lee wanted his jury trial protections incorporated at every possible point.

After agreeing to report the committee bill, Richard Henry Lee then leveled an Antifederalist attack at the jurisdiction of the district courts. On the opening day of debate, June 22, Lee moved to limit the district courts to admiralty jurisdiction. Simply stated, Lee's proposed amendment called for the judiciaries of the several states to serve as lower federal courts in most instances. While many people believed that state courts could handle the business that might be assigned to lower federal courts, opponents of this view argued that state control over the application of federal law would result in diminished popular confidence that national laws were being executed impartially. State judges who held office only for specified terms could not be relied upon to be independent, and appeals to the Supreme Court would have to be allowed in large numbers of cases to ensure the enforcement of national interests. Moreover, some argued that as soon as state judges exercised federal powers, they would become federal judges, with life tenure and secure salaries as mandated by the second clause of Article III, Section 1. Why Lee chose to introduce his amendment after apparently having gone along with the committee in setting up a lower court sytem is not known. Perhaps Lee felt obligated to bring this proposal to the attention of the full Senate because he had been so directed by the Virginia legislature. The oddity is increased by the fact that Virginia had just enacted a restriction on its courts forbidding them to try causes arising under the laws of the United States.

Even Maclay, who had been on the committee with Lee and who would join Lee in voting against the bill in its final form, did not support Lee on this point. Maclay joined with the Federalists in believing that the Constitution's scheme would be thwarted unless the federal courts could adjudicate other issues besides admiralty—such as taxation, duties and imports, naturalization, coinage, counterfeiting, and treason. He also made the long-standing Federalist point that the state judges would not enforce federal laws. William Paterson may have advanced some of the additional reasons against using state courts as federal tribunals: his personal notes reflect that he thought the elective office of most state judges was not compatible with the constitutional requirements of tenure during good behavior and fixed salaries. Paterson agreed that state judges should not be relied upon to enforce federal criminal laws or the collection of federal revenue. The Federalist majority, many of whom had already rejected the notion of state courts as lower federal courts in their correspondence with constituents, followed this view.

The Bill of Rights

At the same time that the Senate was considering the judiciary bill, the House had taken up the subject of a bill of rights. As originally proposed by James Madison on June 6, it included several amendments pertainining to the judicial system. Deemed most important were those protecting the rights of the criminally accused: the right to grand jury indictment, to a speedy and public trial by an impartial jury of the vicinage, to know the cause and nature of accusations, to confront witnesses and have compulsory process to produce them, to assistance of counsel, to due process, and to protection against self-incrimination, double jeopardy, excessive bail, fines, and cruel and unusual punishment. With the exception of the jury of the vicinage, which was struck by the Senate, all of these became parts of the Fifth, Sixth and Eighth Amendments. Madison's list also included the three judicial system amendments considered most important by the Antifederalists: a guarantee of jury trial in common law cases (that is, suits governed by earlier judicial decisions rather than by statutes) above twenty dollars; a prohibition on the reexamination of the facts found in a case by the trial court except by the restrictive rules of the common law (which meant that jury decisions would not be easily overturned); and a monetary restriction on all appeals to the Supreme Court. The Senate removed this last provision, but the first two became the Seventh Amendment. The Senate also voted down a requirement for unanimous jury verdicts and the grant of a right to make jury challenges. Moreover, that body refused to agree to what Madison considered the most important of all: a prohibition against state violations of fundamental rights, including trial by jury.

Although Madison had received House approval of his amendments as the only ones to be discussed, members continued to attempt additions. The most extreme judicial amendments offered were those of Thomas Tudor Tucker of South Carolina to limit lower federal courts to admiralty jurisdiction and to prohibit any federal jurisdiction over diversity cases, suits involving foreigners, and suits involving land grants from two different states. Unsuccessful in that effort, Tucker, on the last day of debate again tried, but failed, to limit the lower courts to hearing only admiralty cases.

Having postponed consideration of the judiciary bill until after passage of a bill of rights, the House began debate on the former on August 27. Despite heavy speculation that Madison would lead the attack, he failed to do so, and few substantive changes were made. Tucker renewed his attempts, made without success during the bill of rights debates, to eliminate the district courts. He was joined in this by Samuel Livermore of New Hampshire; their proposal engendered more debate than any other issue, but ultimately went down to defeat. In his closing speech on the bill, delivered on September 17, Madison summed up the views of most of his colleagues that the bill, however imperfect, was the best they could get at this late date in the session, and that it could always be changed as experience proved necessary.

The only direct evidence of interaction between the two houses as they considered the judiciary bill and the bill of rights is a letter of September 24 from Madison to Edmund Pendleton, discussing the bill of rights. "It will be impossible I find to prevail on the Senate to concur in limitation on the value of appeals to the Supreme Court," complained Madison,

which they say is unnecessary, and might be embarrassing in questions of national or Constitutional importance in their principle, tho' of small pecuniary amount. They are equally inflexible in opposing a definition of the locality of Juries. The vicinage they contend is either too vague or too strict, too vague if depending on limits to be fixed by the pleasure of the law, too strict if limited to the County. . . . The Senate suppose also that the provision for vicinage in the Judiciary bill, will sufficiently quiet the fears which called for an amendment on this point.

On September 19, the Senate had proposed a compromise to the judiciary bill which allowed the trial jury in capital cases to be drawn from the county in which the crime was committed. It was adopted by the House on September 21, the same day that a joint conference committee of Representatives Madison, Sherman and Vining, and Senators Ellsworth, Paterson, and Carroll was appointed to resolve the differences over the bill of rights. Three days later on September 24, as the conference committee was agreeing to limit constitutional protection to a jury of the district, President Washington signed the Judiciary Act into law. Although lit-

Etching of the Chamber of the House of Representatives where James Madison presented his Bill of Rights. Courtesy: Library of Congress.

88 tle hard evidence exists to suggest that the Judiciary Act and the Bill of Rights were deliberately fashioned to complement each other, the fact is that together they took care of most Antifederalist concerns about the judiciary under the Constitution.

Probably none of the Judiciary Act's provisions captured the spirit of balancing state and federal interests that informed the creation of the act better than Section 34. The section stipulated, simply enough,

> [t]hat the laws of the several States except where the Constitution, treaties or statutes of the United States shall otherwise require or provide, shall be regarded as rules of decision in trials at common law in the Courts of the United States in cases where they apply.

While the First Congress may well have intended "laws of the several states" merely as a shorthand for all the laws then in effect, including the unwritten common law, it is equally possible that the Framers meant "laws" to refer only to statutes, leaving the federal courts free to fashion common law remedies of their own. Even if the drafters did intend that "laws" include the common law of the several states, they may have wished merely to permit, not to compel, the federal trial courts to apply state common law. Still another possibility is that the bill's framers deliberately worded the provision vaguely so as to leave its meaning open to future judicial interpretation. Its literal meaning notwithstanding, the thirty-fourth section was written, like the other sections, in the spirit of reconciling national interests with those of the various states. The enactment of the Judiciary Act of 1789 marked the culmination of an ef-

Draft of the Judiciary Bill (S-1), June 12, 1789.
Courtesy: Senate Records, National Archives.

fort to implement federal law adequately and yet in a manner least detrimental to state policies and practices.

CONCLUSION

The passage of the Judiciary Act of 1789 was crucial to the growth of the federal judiciary. The remarks of Associate Justice Samuel Chase, in a 1799 opinion, sum up its importance. "The notion has frequently been entertained," noted Chase,

> *that the federal courts derive their judicial power immediately from the Constitution; but the political truth is that the disposal of the judicial power (except in a few specified instances) belongs to Congress. If Congress has given the power to this court, we possess it, not otherwise; and if Congress has not given the power to us or to any other court, it still remains at the legislative disposal.*

The generality of Article III of the Constitution raised questions that Congress had to address in the Judiciary Act of 1789. These questions had no easy answers, and the solutions to them were achieved politically. The First Congress decided that it could regulate the jurisdiction of all federal courts, and in the Judiciary Act of 1789, Congress established with great particularity a limited jurisdiction for the district and circuit courts, gave the Supreme Court the original jurisdiction provided for in the Constitution, and granted the Court appellate jurisdiction in cases from the federal circuit courts and from state courts where those courts' rulings had rejected federal claims. The decision to grant federal courts a jurisdiction more restrictive than that allowed by the Constitution represented a recognition by the Congress that the people of the United States would not find a full-blown federal court system palatable at that time.

For nearly all of the next century, the judicial system remained essentially as established by the Judiciary Act of 1789. Only after the country had expanded across a continent and had been torn apart by civil war were major changes made. A separate tier of appellate circuit courts created in 1891 removed the burden of circuit riding from the shoulders of the Supreme Court justices but otherwise left intact the judicial structure.

With minor adjustments, it is the same system we have today. Congress has continued to build on the interpretation of the drafters of the first judiciary act in exercising a discretionary power to expand or restrict federal court jurisdiction. While opinions as to what constitutes the proper balance of federal and state concerns vary no less today than they did nearly two centuries ago, the fact that today's federal court system closely resembles the one created in 1789 suggests that the First Congress performed its job admirably.

*Reprinted, with permission, from *this Constitution*, No.17, Winter 1987. Washington, D.C.: Project '87, 1987.

John Jay: Federalist and Chief Justice

by Herbert Alan Johnson

As John Jay had emerged as a patriot in the First and Second Continental Congresses, so he was to develop into a Federalist when he participated in the debates of the New York State ratifying convention. There, he along with his Federalist colleagues from New York City, Alexander Hamilton and Robert R. Livingston, championed the new form of government. Gradually they helped convince the opposition to join their camp and finally secured ratification of the document that had been drafted in Philadelphia.

When the new government replaced the old Congress of the Articles of Confederation in March 1789, George Washington requested Jay to remain as secretary for foreign affairs until a successor could be named. President Washington then consulted Jay concerning which office in the new government he would prefer, and after brief hesitation, Jay chose the chief justiceship of the new Supreme Court of the United States. Washington heartily approved his friend's choice, and the man who had been first chief justice of the supreme court of the independent state of New York became, on September 26, 1789, the first chief justice of the United States. At Washington's request, he also continued to act as secretary for foreign affairs until relieved by Washington's appointee, Thomas Jefferson, on March 22, 1790.

In electing to serve as chief justice, John Jay deprived himself of the comforts he had come to enjoy from his residence in New York City. His large town house had served as one of the

Chief Justice John Jay in his judicial robes. Oil on canvas by Keller after Stuart. Courtesy: New York State Office of Parks, Recreation and Historic Preservation.

social centers of the city during Jay's term as secretary for foreign affairs, where he and his wife, Sarah, had many friends. Now as chief justice, he would be required to spend many months of the year riding circuit. The Judiciary Act of 1789 assigned to the Justices of the Supreme Court the duty of sitting in the various circuit courts of the United States. Because the circuit courts were then the principal trial courts in the federal court system, this meant repeated journeys over the poorly maintained highways of the day. Jay's diary concerning his experiences on circuit makes it abundantly clear that he found numerous reasons for hating this portion of his judicial duties. The food in country inns was inevitably poor, lodgings were better than those he had suffered in Spain but much inferior to the comforts of home, and with all of this, he was deprived of the companionship of his wife and young children.

Aside from his personal aversion to these circuit duties, Jay and his associates thought it improper to assign Supreme Court justices to serve as trial judges in the circuit courts, because their decisions in the circuit courts would then be subject to review by the Court of which they were members. All members of the Court wished to see this arrangement remedied. Consequently, the justices petitioned Congress to amend the Judiciary Act so that Supreme Court justices would be relieved of circuit duties. For some time, Congress ignored this request, and only after Jay had resigned from the office of chief justice did Congress pass a law which diminished, but did not eliminate, the circuit duties imposed upon each individual justice.

As the first chief justice of the United States, Jay established the rules of practice before the Court with some degree of assurance because he had been faced with a similar situation when he had become chief justice of New York twelve years earlier. He proposed that the practice of the Court be governed by the rules of the English courts of King's Bench and Chancery. He also fixed the rule, still in effect, that attorneys and counselors be admitted to practice in the high Court only after three years' practice before the highest courts of the state of their residence, and that their professional character be ''fair.'' Perhaps most significant, Jay was instrumental in the Court's refusal to give an advisory opinion to President Washington, thus fixing the precedent of not giving unofficial opinions on matters not at issue before the Supreme Court. Just as Washington conferred upon the office of president many valued customs and traditions, so did John Jay set a pattern to guide the future conduct of the chief justices of the United States Supreme Court.

As peace commissioner and secretary for foreign affairs, Jay had been deeply concerned with the payment of debts owed by Americans to the merchants of Great Britain, and as chief justice he also had to deal with this controversial issue. With the establishment of the federal courts, British creditors could sue American debtors in a circuit court of the United States. Although there were a number of such cases in the federal courts, the first to come to trial was *Ware* v. *Hylton*, scheduled to be heard in the Virginia Circuit Court in 1793. Normally, Jay did not sit on this court, but in 1793 the circuit duties were reallocated so that he presided in Richmond when *Ware* was argued. His very presence was a reminder of the solemn treaty obligations of the United States, and his opinion was a resounding affirmance of the right of British creditors to collect from Virginians. In *Ware,* Jay was outvoted by his fellow Supreme Court justice, James Iredell, and by District Judge Cyrus Griffin. When the case was appealed, the Supreme Court reversed the circuit court in an opinion that upheld Jay's reasoning. By that time, Jay had left the Court, and in the interim had negotiated another treaty with Britain on the problem of British debts.

In another important case, Jay and his colleagues settled, temporarily, a vexing problem of state sovereignty. This was the case of *Chisholm* v. *Georgia* (1793), in which the State of Georgia was sued in the Supreme Court of the United States for a debt incurred by the state legislature during the American Revolution. The creditor, a South Carolina merchant, had sold arms to Georgia, but after the war the state refused to pay, and his estate brought an action in the Supreme Court. The governor and attorney general of Georgia refused to appear before the Court. After some hesitation, the justices held that Georgia was subject to the jurisdiction of the Court, and ordered her to pay. Georgia refused, and because the Supreme Court lacked enforcement power, the South Carolinian's estate never collected.

John Jay's opinion supporting the Supreme Court's jurisdiction over Georgia is worthy of attention, for it is the clearest statement of his views on state sovereignty. Lest the assumption be made that his viewpoint was affected

Marble bust of John Jay by Ottavio Giovannozzi, 1827. Courtesy: New York State Office of Parks, Recreation and Historic Preservation.

because Georgia was the defendant, it should be noted that he held similar views in *Oswald* v. *New York*, which involved his own state as a party defendant.

The chief justice began his opinion in *Chisholm* by flatly rejecting the claim that Georgia had sovereign immunity against Chisholm's action. Sovereign immunity, he pointed out, is a rule that protects a state from being sued by its subjects without state consent. In Georgia's case, there was no such immunity, nor did any other American state possess sovereignty in the years from 1776 to 1789. Rather, the sovereign power which in the colonial period had rested in the Crown of Great Britain, had passed to the United States in Congress assembled, and had been exercised by that federal body on behalf of all the American people. State officers, Jay pointed out, were mere agents of a sovereign people, and as such were not immune from suit. Clearly, sovereign immunity was alien to the American concept of government and inappropriate regarding state government and officials.

Jay's vision of a federal union predicated on law is obvious from his comments in *Chisholm*. His concept of republican government mandated a ''state of society that was so far improved and the science of government advanced to such a degree of perfection, as that the whole nation could in the peaceable course of law, be compelled to do justice, and be sued by individual citizens.'' Equity and justice supported

Jay's signature and engraving. Courtesy: New York State Office of Parks, Recreation and Historic Preservation.

the extension of federal judicial power to *Chisholm,* for this jurisdiction "performs the promise which every free government makes to every free citizen, of equal justice and protection... because it recognizes and strongly rests on this great moral truth, that justice is the same whether due from one man or a million, or from a million to one man...." Concluded Jay, "it brings into action, and enforces this great and glorious principle that the people are the sovereigns of this country and consequently that fellow citizens and joint sovereigns cannot be degraded by appearing with each other in their own courts to have their controversies determined."

This generous and broad view of the sovereignty of the people and moral authority of the Supreme Court under the Constitution was, as noted, ignored by the State of Georgia. Even while *Chisholm* was being argued before the Court, the Eleventh Amendment to the Federal Constitution had been drafted in Congress, and after the Court's opinions were read, was sent to the states for ratification. In 1798, the requisite number of states had ratified and the amendment became law. Thereafter, no state could be sued by the citizens of any other state in the United States Supreme Court. Jay's expansive view of the federal union ruled by law had enjoyed a five-year existence.

The chief justice's participation in the Court's decision of *Chisholm* was in many ways a turning point in his career as well as in the history of the United States. By the time he wrote his opinion in 1793, the nationalism expressed in his words had already begun to erode away into the divisive doctrine of states' rights. While Jay and his fellow Federalists sought vigorous government at the national level, opponents hoped to weaken the federal government while strengthening the independence and self-determination of the individual states. John Jay belonged to the generation that had guided the American states through the Revolutionary War. He understood well the threat of disunion, and his lawyer's sense of equity and justice was repelled by state governments treating their creditors with disdain. In the political arena of the 1790s, Jay was part of a rapidly shrinking minority of Federalist political leaders, and even his insistence upon justice for all men was to result in calumny for himself and political defeats for his party. A man of firm and inflexible principle, Jay remained steadfast in his support of the national state he believed to be essential to American prosperity.

*Adapted, with permission, from Herbert Alan Johnson, *John Jay: 1745-1829.* (Albany, NY: New York State Office of History, 1970), 35-39.

FOR FURTHER READING

Charles F. Hobson, et al., eds., *The Papers of John Marshall.* 5 vols. to date. Chapel Hill: University of North Carolina Press, 1974-____. See vol. 5, 259-263, 295-329.

Clyde E. Jacobs, *The Eleventh Amendment and Sovereign Immunity.* Westport, Conn.: Greenwood Press, 1972.

Frank Monaghan, *John Jay.* New York: Bobbs-Merrill Co., 1935.

Richard B. Morris, *John Jay, the Nation and the Court.* Boston: Boston University Press, 1967.

Congress Proposes the Bill of Rights

by John P. Kaminski

On March 4, 1789, the new Congress under the Constitution began assembling. In his inaugural address of April 30, President George Washington recommended that Congress consider possible amendments to the Constitution. Instead of proposing specific amendments, Washington felt confident that Congress would "carefully avoid every alteration which might endanger the benefits of an United and effective Government, or which ought to await the future lessons of experience." On the other hand, "a reverence for the characteristic rights of freemen, and a regard for the public harmony" should influence Congress' consideration.[1]

Federalists worried that the states might require Congress to call a second general convention to amend the Constitution. Such a convention, proposed by New York's ratifying convention, would be unrestricted in the amendments it could propose. Perhaps, in fact, an entirely new constitution might be recommended as was done by the Federal Convention in 1787. This fear intensified when Virginia on November 20, 1788, and New York on February 7, 1789, petitioned Congress for another convention.

On May 4, 1789, James Madison notified his fellow congressmen that he intended to introduce amendments to the Constitution later in the month. The next day, Madison's Virginia colleague, Theodorick Bland, presented to the U.S. House of Representatives his state's call for a second general convention. (According to James Monroe, "the draft was revised and corrected by

James Madison dealt with measures that created the executive department, formed the judiciary, established the revenue system, and framed the Bill of Rights. Oil on canvas by Charles Willson Peale. Courtesy: Thomas Gilcrease Institute of American History and Art.

98 Bland and partakes of his usual fire and elegance.'')[2] The people of Virginia and of the other states believed that the Constitution endangered ''all the great and unalienable rights of freemen.'' The objections to the Constitution ''were not founded in speculative theory, but (were) deduced from principles which have been established by the melancholy example of other nations in different ages.'' Expected to be busy setting up the new government, Congress would surely act slowly in making recommendations for amendments. Thus, Virginia felt obliged to have Congress call a second constitutional convention. New York echoed Virginia's request when on May 6, Representative John Laurance of New York City presented his state's request for another convention.[3]

On Monday, June 8, 1789, Madison, fulfilling the wishes of his state's ratifying convention and his election promise to his constituents, and also trying to defuse the Antifederalists' attempt to call a second constitutional convention, asked the House of Representatives to go into a committee of the whole to consider amendments to the Constitution. Opponents of the measure suggested that the House propose either a select committee to consider amendments or Madison propose his amendments, have them printed and distributed to the members, and then assign a date for later discussion. An immediate consideration of amendments appeared to be ''premature.'' More important matters in setting up

the government should first be considered. Even supporters of amendments believed that the time had not yet arrived to consider the subject. Madison reluctantly agreed that it was inopportune for Congress to consider amendments immmediately, but he presented his amendments so that they could be submitted to a committee for later debate by Congress. ''Prudence,'' however, Madison said, dictated that before the end of its first session, Congress submit amendments to the state legislatures.

Madison believed that ''a great number'' of Americans were ''dissatisfied'' with the Constitution. ''On the principles of amity and moderation,'' he wished to protect expressly ''the great rights of mankind'' under the Constitution. Such an act might also convince North Carolina and Rhode Island to join the Union. Above all, however, Madison believed that all power is subject to abuse; therefore, it would be proper to guard more adequately against this dangerous potential. He agreed that the door should not

Right: *In New York, Albany's mayor, John Lansing, Jr., supported the drive for a bill of rights. From* The Critical Period, *Fiske.*
Far right: *Title page of Mary Wollstonecraft's epic work,* A Vindication of the Rights of Woman. *This feminist declaration of independence was published in 1792, when revolution was fresh in American minds and still gripped the French nation. Courtesy: New York State Library, Manuscripts and Special Collections Division.*

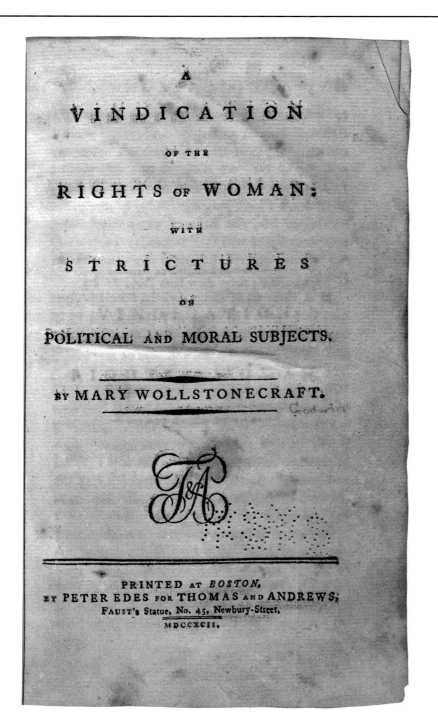

A

VINDICATION

OF THE

RIGHTS OF WOMAN:

WITH

STRICTURES

ON

POLITICAL AND MORAL SUBJECTS.

BY MARY WOLLSTONECRAFT.

PRINTED AT *BOSTON*,
BY PETER EDES FOR THOMAS AND ANDREWS,
FAUST's Statue, No. 45, Newbury-Street.
MDCCXCII.

be opened to "a reconsideration of the whole structure of the Government," but a consideration of "the security of rights" posed no danger to the new federal government.

Madison thought that the majority of Antifederalists opposed the Constitution because they feared the possible "encroachments on particular rights," especially in those cases where Americans had become accustomed to "safeguards...interposed between them and the magistrate who exercises the sovereign power." Consequently, Madison proposed a number of amendments to the Constitution which, taken together, made up a bill of rights. He stated that he never believed that a bill was so essential that the Constitution should be rejected until one was added. He stressed that his amendments would not affect "the structure and stamina of the government" but would be "important in the eyes of many" as the protection they had sought during the ratification debate. Amendments protecting fundamental rights would prove that Federalists were "sincerely devoted to liberty and a republican government." And, while it was true that bills of rights in Great Britain "have gone no farther than to raise a barrier against the power of the Crown" while the power of the legislature is left unchecked, in America the people "have thought it necessary to raise barriers against power in all forms and departments of Government." The great object in Madison's view was "to limit and qualify the powers of Government, by excepting out of the grant of power those cases in which the Government ought not to act, or to act only in a particular mode."

Many people thought these amendments were unnecessary. Noah Webster, writing as "A Free Mechanic" in the *New York Journal*, August 20, 1789, attacked Madison's proposal: "It seems to be agreed on all hands that paper declarations of rights are trifling things and no real security to liberty.'' But Madison believed that paper declarations would ''have a tendency to impress some degree of respect for them, to establish the public opinion in their favor, and rouse the attention of the whole community.''

Ardent Antifederalists throughout the country who had advocated both a bill of rights and significant structural changes to the Constitution denounced Madison's amendments. George Mason of Virginia characterized Madison as a supporter of ''Milk & Water Propositions'' that would serve as ''a Tub to the Whale,'' that is, a diversion from significant alterations.[4] Other Virginians viewed the amendments ''as an anodyne to the discontented'' or ''as a soporific draught to the restless.[5] South Carolina Antifederalist Aedanus Burke condemned the amendments in Congress as ''frothy and full of wind, formed only to please the palate.''[6] Pennsylvania Congressman George Clymer likened Madison to ''a sensible physician he had given his malades imaginaries bread pills powder of paste &c neutral mixtures to keep them in play.''[7]

Ironically, Madison now answered all those arguments against bills of rights previously put forth by Federalists (which he had led) during the ratification debate. Over and over again, Madison said that Federalist disclaimers against a bill of rights were inconclusive. Furthermore, a bill of rights incorporated into a constitution would empower the independent judicial tribunals to consider themselves ''in a peculiar manner the guardians of those rights; they will be an impenetrable bulwark against every assumption of power in the legislature or executive.''

Congress divided, sometimes bitterly, over Madison's amendments. James Jackson of Georgia dismissed them as ''theoretical speculation.'' If ''not dangerous or improper,'' Madison's amendments were ''at least unnecessary.'' Elbridge Gerry of Massachusets, however, felt that it would be ''improper'' to consider Madison's few amendments, when there were many other substantial amendments proposed by the state conventions. Antifederalists would lose faith in Congress if only Madison's amendments were considered. On some occasions, the intensity of the debate reached the point where congressmen were ready to settle their disagreements on the dueling field, but cooler heads prevailed, and no duels were fought.[8] The debates on June 8 ended when Congress agreed that Madison's amendments should, at some future date, be considered in the committee of the whole.

On July 21, six weeks after Madison had first introduced his amendments, he ''begged the House to indulge him'' in their further consideration. The House voted to send Madison's amendments and all of the other amendments submitted by state ratifying conventions to a select committee composed of one member from each state. A week later, on July 28, the committee reported a list of seventeen amendments—basically a composite of Madison's amendments— which were ordered to lie on the table. On August 3, Madison again urged the House to take up the amendments, and it was agreed to discuss the committee's report on August 12. Other business occupied the House on the twelfth, and thus the discussion was postponed. On the thirteenth, a lengthy debate occurred on the propriety of considering amendments when other more pressing matters awaited the House's consideration. Madison saw the real possibility that amendments would not be proposed during this first session of Congress. He pleaded with the House:

> I admit, with the worthy gentlemen who preceded me, that a great number of the community are solicitous to see the Government carried into operation; but I believe that there is a considerable part also anxious to secure those rights which they are apprehensive are endangered by the present constitution. Now, considering the full confidence they reposed at the time of its adoption in their future representatives, I think we ought to pursue the subject to effect.

The House voted to accede to Madison's wishes, and between August 13 and 24, the amendments were debated first in a committee of the whole and then after August 18 in the House itself.

At times during this debate, Madison's amendments appeared to be dead because they did not have the support of the necessary two-thirds majority required by Article V of the Constitution. Madison asked President Washington for support. Washington responded by stating that some of the amendments were ''importantly necessary'' while others, though not essential in his judgment, would be ''necessary to quiet the fears of some respectable characters and well meaning Men. Upon the whole, therefore, not foreseeing any evil consequences that can result from their adoption, they have my wishes for a favorable reception in both houses."[9] With Washington's support, the amendments were approved by the House of Representatives.

One important decision that some representatives at the time thought "trifling" was the matter of form. How would amendments be added to the Constitution? Would they be placed at the end of the original document or would they be interspersed throughout, deleting passages of the original Constitution that were no longer applicable and altering others? Madison urged the latter, arguing that "there is a neatness and propriety in incorporating the amendments into the Constitution itself." The Constitution, he argued, would "certainly be more simple, when the amendments are interwoven into those parts to which they naturally belong, than it will if they consist of separate and distinct parts." Roger Sherman of Connecticut opposed this interweaving, arguing that "We might as well endeavor to mix brass, iron, and clay, as to incorporate such heterogeneous articles." James Jackson advocated "that the original constitution ought to remain inviolate, and not be patched up, from time to time, with various stuffs resembling Joseph's coat of many colors." On August 13, Madison's arrangement was approved, only to be overturned by a two-thirds vote six days later.

On August 24, 1789, the House of Representatives sent seventeen proposed amendments to the Senate. The Senate read the amendments on the twenty-fifth, when Ralph Izard of South Carolina, John Langdon of New Hampshire, and Robert Morris of Pennsylvania treated them "contemptuously." Izard and Langdon unsuccessfully moved to postpone their consideration to the next session, and on September 2, the Senate began its consideration of the amendments. Within three weeks, the Senate had tightened the language and consolidated the amendments into a list of twelve, which the Senate approved. Significantly, the Senate eliminated the amendment which Madison considered "the most valuable amendment in the whole lot" when it struck out the prohibition on the

states from infringing on the freedom of conscience, speech, press and jury trial. (This omission was a harbinger of the decision by the United States Supreme Court in the 1833 case *Barron* v. *Baltimore*, in which the Bill of Rights was declared applicable only to the federal government, not to the states.) After rejecting a host of amendments based on the Virginia ratifying convention's recommendations, the Senate adopted its version of amendments on September 9, 1789.

The House of Representatives received the Senate's amendments on September 10. It agreed to some of the Senate's changes, and on September 21, called a conference committee to settle the differences. The committee—composed of Madison, Sherman, and John Vining from the House, and Oliver Ellsworth, Charles Carroll, and William Paterson from the Senate—reported to the House of Representatives on September 23. The following day, the House accepted the committee's report by a vote of 37 to 14, and passed a resolution requesting President Washington to transmit copies of the proposed amendments to the eleven states in the Union as well as to North Carolina and Rhode Island. On September 25, the Senate concurred with the House of Representatives. Congress had complied with the provisions of Article V of the Constitution in recommending amendments to the state legislatures. It acted to satisfy the ap-

Senator William Paterson of New Jersey served on the committee that prepared the judiciary bill. From the original by Sharples. Courtesy: Independence National Historical Park.

prehensions raised by Antifederalists throughout the ratification debate.

On October 2, 1789, President Washington sent the amendments to the states for their approval. Several state legislatures rejected the first two amendments which provided a formula for the apportionment of the House of Representatives and for a restriction on the power of congressmen to enact salary increases for themselves. It took more than two years for the other ten amendments—the future Bill of Rights—to be adopted by the necessary three-fourths of the state legislatures.

*Excerpted from ''The Adoption of the Bill of Rights'' by John P. Kaminski in Stephen L. Schechter, ed., *Forgotten Partners: The Bill of Rights and the States* (Albany, NY: New York State Bicentennial Commission. Forthcoming.)

[1] Dorothy Twohig, ed. *Presidential Series*, vol. 2, in W.W. Abbot et al., eds., *The Papers of George Washington* (Charlottesville, Va.: University Press of Virginia, 1987), 176.

[2] James Monroe to Thomas Jefferson, Fredericksburg, February 15, 1789, Jefferson Papers, Library of Congress.

[3] All quotations from the congressional debate over the proposed amendments can be found in Bernard Schwartz, ed., *The Roots of The Bill of Rights* (5 vols., New York: Chelsea House, 1971, 1980), vol. 5.

[4] Mason to John Mason, July 31, 1789, Robert A. Rutland, ed., *The Papers of George Mason* (3 vols., Chapel Hill, N.C.: University of North Carolina Press, 1970), 1164.

[5] Edmund Randolph to James Madison, Williamsburg, June 30, 1789. Robert A. Rutland, ed., *The Papers of James Madison*, 12: (Charlottesville, Va., 1979), 273.

[6] Quoted in Kenneth R. Bowling, ''A Tub to the Whale': The Founding Fathers and Adoption of the Federal Bill of Rights,'' *The Journal of the Early Republic*, 8 (Fall 1989), 241.

[7] George Clymer to Tench Coxe, New York, June 28, 1789, Coxe Papers, Tench Coxe Section, Historical Society of Pennsylvania.

[8] Elbridge Gerry to Samuel R. Gerry, New York, June 30, 1790, Samuel Russel Gerry Papers, Massachusetts Historical Society.

[9] Washington to Madison, n.d., Rutland, *Madison*, 12: 191.

FOR FURTHER READING

Kenneth R. Bowling '''A Tub to the Whale': The Founding Fathers and Adoption of the Bill of Rights.'' *The Journal of the Early Republic*, 8 (Fall 1989), 223-51. Published for the Society for Historians of the Early American Republic. Indianapolis: Indiana University/Purdue University, 1989.

Edward Dumbauld, *The Bill of Rights and What It Means Today*. University of Oklahoma Press, Norman, Okla.: 1957.

Jon Kukla ed., *The Bill of Rights: A Lively Heritage*. Richmond: Virginia State Library and Archives, 1987.

Leonard W. Levy, ed., *Encyclopedia of the American Constitution*. 4 vols. New York: Macmillan, 1986.

Robert A. Rutland, *The Birth of the Bill of Rights, 1776-1791*. Chapel Hill, N.C.: University of North Carolina Press, 1955.

Bernard Schwartz, *The Great Rights of Mankind: A History of the American Bill of Rights*. New York: Oxford University Press, 1977.

EPILOGUE

The Centennial Commemoration of George Washington's Inauguration

by Richard B. Bernstein

The celebration in 1889 of the 100th anniversary of George Washington's inauguration and the launching of government under the Constitution was one of the most elaborate and spectacular historical commemorations in the nation's history.[1]

On March 4, 1884, plans to observe the centennial began with resolutions adopted by a formal meeting at The New-York Historical Society; the society took the initiative in targeting the anniversary as worthy of commemoration. (In 1839, the Historical Society sponsored the only formal commemoration of the fiftieth anniversary, hosting a formal dinner at which former President John Quincy Adams of Massachusetts delivered a two-hour ''historical discourse'' entitled *The Jubilee of the Constitution*.[2]) Similar resolutions were adopted by the New York Society of the Sons of the Revolution in 1885 and the New York Chamber of Commerce in 1886.

The Committee of Citizens, which became the focus of centennial planning, was organized at a meeting at the Fifth Avenue Hotel on November 10, 1887, presided over by the mayor of New York City, Abram S. Hewitt. Mayor Hewitt appointed an executive committee of thirteen citizens, known as the Committee of Thirteen, which coordinated activities with the committees of The New-York Historical Society, the Chamber of Commerce, and the Sons of the Revolution. On December 7, 1887, these committees merged as the Committee of Citizens, which then conducted its activities and prepared and

Former Presidents Rutherford B. Hayes and Grover Cleveland proceeding from the Sub-Treasury to the grandstand to review the grand military parade, April 30, 1889. (Cleveland is clearly visible, seated in the coach; Hayes is obscured by the coachman's elbow.) Courtesy: New York City Commission on the Bicentennial of the Constitution.

carried out plans as a unified body.

The Committee of Citizens (the General Committee) appointed eleven committees—Plan and Scope, States, General Government, Army (Military and Industrial Parade), Navy, Entertainment, Finance, Railroads and Transportation, Art, Exhibition, and Literary Exercises. (Art and Exhibition were later merged as one committee.) As noted in the official history of the centennial observances, ''So great was the pressure to join the General Committee, that the number was finally limited to two hundred.''[3]

The finance committee of the Committee of Citizens undertook to raise $175,000—$75,000 from New York City, $55,000 from New York State, and $45,000 from private fund-raising. New York State appropriated $200,000 to help defray the cost of the commemoration—$125,000 for the National Guard, $20,000 for the Grand Army of the Republic (the veterans of the Union Army in the Civil War), and $55,000 for the Committee of Citizens in New York City.[4]

The centennial celebrations focused on the three days April 29 to May 1, 1889. Two other events served as a prelude and complement to the main program:

■ An exhibition of historical portraits and artifacts from the period 1776-1789 was organized in the spring of 1888 and was held for six weeks in the old Metopolitan Opera House, opening to the public on April 3, 1889.

President Benjamin Harrison delivering remarks at the literary exercises at the Sub-Treasury, April 30, 1889. (Harrison is the bearded man standing next to the flagpole.) Courtesy: New York City Commission on the Bicentennial of the Constitution.

■ A commemorative banquet sponsored by the Society of the Cincinnati was held at the Lawyers' Club in the old Equitable Building on the evening of April 27, 1889. One of the guests of honor was former President Rutherford B. Hayes of Ohio.

The president of the United States, Benjamin Harrison of Indiana, and his vice president, Levi P. Morton of New York, played leading roles in the events of April 29 to May 1, 1889. In part, this was because all participants in the commemoration wanted it to be a national rite of reconciliation to end the bitterness and recriminations resulting from the experience of the Civil War. In part, it was also the result of Harrison's natural desire to cement his political legitimacy in the eyes of the American people; he had won the 1888 presidential election, unseating the incumbent, Grover Cleveland of New York, by amassing more electoral votes than Cleveland in the Electoral College, even though Cleveland had outpolled him in the popular vote.

Joining Harrison and Morton and former Presidents Cleveland and Hayes were representatives of the U.S. Supreme Court (including newly appointed Chief Justice Melville W. Fuller of Maine), delegations from the House of Representatives and the Senate, members of Harrison's Cabinet (representing the executive departments of government), the diplomatic corps, and delegations from every state in the Union (including, in most cases, the states' governors).

The various representatives of the federal government, led by the president and vice president, made a ceremonial trip from Washington, D.C., to New York City. They intended to follow exactly the route followed by George Washington on his journey from his Virginia plantation, Mount Vernon, to

New York City, but constraints of time forced them to abridge the schedule. Instead, they departed in a special train from Washington, D.C., on the evening of April 28, 1889. The presidential party arrived in Elizabeth, New Jersey, on April 29; the site was picked because George Washington had departed from Elizabethtown (as it was then named) for New York City a century before.

The first major event of the centennial commemoration was the president's reprise on April 29 of Washington's trip across New York harbor (on the morning of April 23, 1789). After a breakfast with Governor Robert S. Green of New Jersey, the presidential party was conducted by military escort to Elizabethport. The U.S.S. *Despatch* picked up the presidential party (a second steamer, the U.S.S. *Sirius*, took on others who could not be accommodated on the *Despatch*). A barge (reproducing that which carried George Washington from Elizabethport to New York City in 1789) crewed by ship masters of the New York Marine Society, the same organization that had conducted Washington, met the *Despatch*. President Harrison and Vice President Morton transferred to the barge to be rowed across the harbor to the foot of Wall Street, landing at what was then Pier 16 (renumbered since then as the present Pier 11).

During this event, the harbor swarmed with ships and boats of every size and description. A grand naval parade, divided into two sections—naval and merchant marine—took place. The naval parade included the cruisers U.S.S. *Chicago*, U.S.S. *Boston*,

and U.S.S. *Yorktown*, and the steamers U.S.S. *Atlanta*, U.S.S *Juniata*, and U.S.S *Yantic*, followed by a procession of revenue cutters and yachts. The merchant marine section comprised about three hundred ships of all descriptions (mostly river and harbor steamers), organized into twenty-three divisions of thirteen ships each; these divisions were formed into three grand divisions, each commanded by a specially appointed "commodore." Great attention was paid to the arrangement of types of vessels, the "dressing" of all ships and boats, and the use of signals, whistles, and other formalities in both parts of the naval parade. As has become traditional in events in New York harbor, the steam tugs also saluted the president and vice president as they were rowed across the harbor. The president and vice president were received on Manhattan by the chairman of the centennial committee, Hamilton Fish, and by Governor David B. Hill of New York and Mayor Hugh L. Grant of New York City. The official centennial history commented on the occasion:

> Never before in the history of the United States had so many vessels been assembled at once in any of its ports to participate in any celebration. Steamers came from many places on the Hudson and Long Island Sound and on the Atlantic seaboard, laden with persons desirous of witnessing the naval review; but amid all the thousands on the waters of New York Bay during that fair day, not an accident occured to mar the general joy. How different the sight from that of a century before, when President Washington came from Elizabethport in a barge through the Kill Van Kull. Then the United States had no navy, and the only naval salutes fired were from the Spanish corvette Galveston and a merchant-ship;

while the only vessels to be seen other than these were a line of barges propelled by oars following in the wake of the President's and a few sloops of small tonnage. The contrast marked the progress of the United States in population, wealth, prosperity, and influence among the nations of the earth. [5]

Following the president's and vice president's landing at the foot of Wall Street, an elaborate march up Wall Street took place. The march, which included delegations from most of the states and territories, ended with a formal reception (for four thousand guests) at the Lawyers' Club in the Equitable Building that afternoon. The various dignitaries enjoyed a banquet at the Lawyers' Club—one for the president and one for the governors of the states—and then took part in a second march to City Hall. After this reception, the president, vice president, and governor were given some time off until the Centennial Ball, which took place that evening at the Metropolitan Opera House and attracted more than seven thousand guests—and, apparently, made a sizeable profit.

On April 30, 1889, the focus of the celebrations, the formal events began with a commemorative religious service at St. Paul's Chapel, the church where Washington worshipped following his swearing in and the only building in lower Manhattan surviving from the 1780s.[6] To mark the occasion, a commemorative bronze tablet was commissioned by the Committee of Citizens and unveiled on Sunday, December 7, 1890.

What were termed "the Literary Exercises at the Sub-Treasury"—known today as Federal Hall National Memorial—then took place. These exercises began with a formal prayer, continued with the oration of the day, delivered delivered by the noted speaker Chaun-

cey M. Depew, and concluded with brief remarks by the president and a closing prayer. A special platform was constructed over the steps of Federal Hall to accommodate the speakers and guests.[7] The crowds extended down Broad, Wall, and Nassau streets. There was no attempt to re-enact the original swearing in of George Washington on this occasion.

Following these exercises, the principal dignitaries were taken to a reviewing stand at Madison Square to review the Grand Military Parade, which proceeded from Wall Street up to Fifty-Ninth Street and Fifth Avenue. The official centennial history estimated that 49,861 men took part—"the largest body of troops ever brought together in this country in time of peace."[8] The ranks of the parade included thirty

governors; 1,168 soldiers from the U.S. Army; 394 U.S. Marines; 1,131 sailors from the U.S. Navy; 288 cadets from the U.S. Military Academy at West Point; 37,785 men from the various detachments of the states' National Guard, state military units, and volunteer militia; 11,876 "Comrades of the Grand Army of the Republic of the United State"—Civil War veterans who had been noncommissioned officers and

---

Left: *President Benjamin Harrison and Vice President Levi P. Morton being rowed to the foot of Wall Street during the naval parade, April 29, 1889. Courtesy: New York City Commission on the Bicentennial of the Constitution.*
Below: *The exhibit of the* New York World *passes the grandstand during the civic and industrial parade, New York, May 1, 1889. Courtesy: New York City Commission on the Bicentennial of the Constitution.*

110 enlisted men; and 200 "Companions of the Military Order of the Loyal Legion of the United States"—Civil War veterans who had been officers of the Union Army. The march moved at the rate of "seven thousand troops per hour" without difficulty or incident: *While the parade was in progress communication was maintained throughout all its parts by telegraph.... The pageant of April 30th...demonstrated to the world the effectiveness of the citizen soldiery of the United States and the ease and rapidity with which fifty thousand men could be mobilized at any given point....*[9]

On the evening of April 30, 1889, a concert at Madison Square took place, in which two thousand singers from forty-five German singing societies performed for a crowd of 50,000 people. The evening concluded with a formal banquet for 800 guests at the Metropolitan Opera House, and with a spectacular display of fireworks by the Unexcelled Fireworks Company at twelve sites throughout Manhattan. "Not a single accident, not a premature explosion, marred the success of the fireworks exhibition."[10]

On May 1, 1889, a second parade—the Civil and Industrial Parade—took place, beginning at Fifty-Ninth Street and Fifth Avenue and continuing down to Canal Street and Broadway. The official history described this event as "a pageant of peace, which exhibited the progress of a century in the industrial arts." It continued: "[O]n May 1st, every trade, every art, every nation, and every representative body of men contributed its brightest and best to make the civic parade an honor to the city of New York."[11] The parade was arranged in ten divisions, each commanded by a marshal. Among the organizations and institutions represented in the parade were: Columbia College, the College of the City of New York, the Hebrew Benevolent and Orphan Asylum, the Bartholdi Battalion of Grammar School No. 15 of Brooklyn, the Knights of Temperance, the Knights of Pythias, the city's volunteer firemen, the New York Fire Department, the Tammany Society, the Manhattan Ship Joiners, the Operative Plasterers' Society, the Brooklyn Plumbers' and Gas-fitters' Union, the Carpenters and Joiners of America, the United Italian Societies, various organizations representing the German-American citizens, organizations representing Irish-American citizens, the United Polish Societies, and "the Colored Centennial Committee." This event concluded the formal commemoration of the centennial. The November 1889 finance committee report indicated that the celebration retained a positive balance of $4,741.09.

Although New York City was the focus of the centennial commemoration, celebrations were also held in Brooklyn, New York; Boston, Worcester, and

The banquet at the Lawyer's Club, Equitable Building, New York City, April 29, 1889. Courtesy: New York City Commission on the Bicentennial of the Constitution.

Pittsfield, Massachusetts; Philadelphia, Pennsylvania; Washington, D.C.; Alexandria and Lexington, Virginia; Birmingham and Selma, Alabama; New Orleans, Louisiana; St. Louis, Missouri; Salt Lake City and Ogden, Utah; Virginia City, Nevada; Tucson, Arizona Territory; Portland, Oregon; Los Angeles, Eureka, and San Francisco, California; the American Church in Paris, France; and the American College in Rome, Italy. Chicago, Illinois, mounted ''[t]he largest celebration… outside of New York.''[12]

The lasting monument of the centennial is Washington Square Arch. A temporary wooden arch had been built for the centennial commemoration. It was so admired that a permanent version was proposed at a formal meeting of the Centennial Committee on Art and Exhibition on May 2, 1889. Ground was broken on April 30, 1890, a year to the day after the centennial. By May 30, 1890, when the cornerstone was laid, subscriptions had reached $106,021.26, with a balance of $9,978.84 needed to complete the arch. The arch was completed in 1895.

In retrospect, the commemoration of the centennial was remarkably characteristic of its time. The prosperous members of the Committee of Citizens and their favored guests saw George Washington almost as one of their own—a wealthy businessman-politician virtually indistinguishable from Andrew Carnegie, Cornelius Vanderbilt, or J.P. Morgan. As we have seen, the centennial was also the occasion for a popular outpouring of patriotic fervor and Washington idolatry, but these celebrations, largely the work of recent immigrants, were at best tolerated by those in charge of the formal program. Thus, the commemoration of the centennial reflected the divided state of American

society in the Gilded Age as much as it did the general veneration of George Washington and the American experiment in government.

[1] The basis of this account is the volume commissioned by the Centennial Committee's Committee on Publications: Clarence W Bowen, ed., *The History of the Centennial Celebration of the Inauguration of George Washington as First President of the United States* (New York: D. Appleton & Co., 1892). This official Centennial history was published in a limited edition of 1,000 copies. (Cited as Bowen, ed., *Centennial History*.) See also chapter 4 of an important new study of George Washington's image in America popular culture: Karal Ann Marling, *George Washington Slept Here* (Cambridge, Mass.: Harvard University Press, 1988). Barry Schwartz, *George Washington: The Making of an American Symbol* (New York: Free Press, 1987), gives a more general interpretation of Washington as an American symbol.

[2] John Quincy Adams, *The Jubilee of the Constitution* (New York: Samuel Colman, 1839). Pp. 121-136 present an account by an anonymous writer of the events of which Adam's ''discourse'' was the centerpiece. See also Bowen, ed., *Centennial History*, 95-99.

[3] Bowen, ed., *Centennial History*, 100-131 (quote at 112).

[4] We have been able to ascertain two estimates for converting 1889 dollar figures into modern, *i.e.*, 1988, terms. According to calculations performed by Mr. Adrian Cooper of the U.S. Department of Commerce for Marjorie Mortensen of the New York City Mayor's Office of Special Projects and Events, one 1889 dollar equals $12.50 in 1988 purchasing power. According to the Economics and Public Affairs Division of the New York Public Library, one 1889 U.S. dollar would equal about $10 in 1988 purchasing power. The Library based its calculations on the November 1987 *Standard and Poor Trading and Securities Statistics*, according to which $1 as of 1889 equaled $3.704 as of 1967, and $1 as of November 1987 equaled $0,312 as of 1967.

[5] Bowen, ed., *Centennial History*, 204-205. See generally *Id.* at 189-205.

[6] The full text of the service is reprinted in Bowen, ed., *Centennial History*, 268-284.

[7] The full text of the speeches, remarks, hymns, and prayers comprising the Literary Exercises may be found in Bowen, ed., *Centennial History*, 285-309.

[8] Bowen, ed., *Centennial History*, 312. See generally *Id.* at 310-349.

[9] Bowen, ed., *Centennial History*, 315, 383.

[10] Bowen, ed., *Centennial History*, 352-353 (quote at 353).

[11] Bowen, ed., *Centennial History*, 383. See generally *Id.* at 383-397.

[12] Bowen, ed., *Centennial History*, 402-406 (quote at 405).

FOR FURTHER READING
Clarence W. Bowen, ed., *The History of the Centennial Celebration of the Inauguration of George Washington as First President of the United States*. New York: D. Appleton & Co., 1892.

Karal Ann Marling, *George Washington Slept Here: Colonial Revivals and American Culture, 1876-1986*. Cambridge, Mass.: Harvard University Press, 1988.

Barry Schwartz, *George Washington: The Making of an American Symbol*. New York: Free Press, 1987.

ABOUT THE AUTHORS

RICHARD ALLAN BAKER is the director of the U.S. Senate Historical Office and served as president of the Society for History in the Federal Government. He is the author of *Conservation Politics: The Senate Career of Clinton P. Anderson* (Albuquerque: University of New Mexico Press, 1985) and *The Senate of the United States: A Bicentennial History* (Malabar, Fla.: Krieger Publishing Company, 1988).

RICHARD B. BERNSTEIN serves as historian to the New York City Bicentennial Commission and is the author (with Kym S. Rice) of the Pulitzer Prize nominee, *Are We To Be A Nation? The Making of the Constitution* (Cambridge, Mass.: Harvard University Press, 1988). Recently published is his three-volume history (with Jerome Agel) of the three branches of the United States government for young readers: *Into The Third Century: The Congress, The Presidency, and The Supreme Court* (New York: Walker, 1989).

CHARLENE BANGS BICKFORD, a colleague of Kenneth R. Bowling at The George Washington University, is co-editor of *The Documentary History of the 1st Federal Congress* (Baltimore: The Johns Hopkins University Press, 1972). A short history of the First Federal Congress by these two authors has been written to accompany an exhibit entitled, ''Birth of a Nation: The First Federal Congress, 1789-1791.''

KENNETH R. BOWLING is currently associated with the First Federal Congress Project at The George Washington University, Washington, D.C., where he is co-editor of *The Documentary History of the 1st Federal Congress.* Volume 9, *The Diary of William Maclay and other Notes on Senate Debates*, was published in 1988.

GORDON DENBOER is the editor of *The Documentary History of the First Federal Elections, 1788-1790*, published by the University of Wisconsin Press, Madison, Wisconsin. Volume 4 is forthcoming. He is also research associate for the Atlas of Historical County Boundaries project at the Newberry Library, Chicago.

JOANNE FREEMAN is presently a consultant at the Library of Congress, where she acts as program coordinator for the Library's Bicentennial of Congress program. She is also researching the life and career of Alexander Hamilton.

HERBERT ALAN JOHNSON is a professor at the University of South Carolina School of Law in Columbia, S.C.

JOHN P. KAMINSKI is the director of the Center for the Study of the American Constitution at the University of Wisconsin, Madison, and co-editor of the *Documentary History of the Ratification of the Constitution* (Madison: University of Wisconsin Press, 1976).

MAEVA MARCUS is director of the Documentary History Project of the United States Supreme Court and editor of *The Documentary History of the Supreme Court of the United States, 1789-1800* (New York: Columbia University Press, 1985). CHRISTINE R. JORDAN is an associate editor of the *History* and holds a Master's degree in American legal history. DAVID EISENBERG was research associate for Marcus at the time the article was written and is now a practicing attorney. EMILY F. VAN TASSEL is currently working on a doctorate in American history. With Marcus, she is the author of "Judges and Legislators in the New Federal System, 1789-1800," in Robert A. Katzmann, ed., *Judges and Legislators: Toward Institutional Comity* (Washington, D.C.: The Brookings Institution, 1988).

RICHARD B. MORRIS was Gouverneur Morris Professor of History at Columbia University and the author of numerous works on early American history. Prior to his death on March 3, 1989, he was engaged in editing *The Papers of John Jay* (New York: Harper & Row, 1975-   ).

JOHN P. RILEY is a research assistant and archivist with The Mount Vernon Ladies' Association of the Union at Mount Vernon, Virginia. His research projects include an exhibit at Mount Vernon entitled, "Federalism—The Great Experiment." Recent publications include an article for *Fairfax Chronicles*, Fairfax County, Virginia, entitled "The Federalist: A 'Specimen of American Ingenuity'" and introductory material for *Maxims of George Washington*, published by The Mount Vernon Ladies' Association (1989).

STEPHEN L. SCHECHTER is executive director of the New York State Bicentennial Commission, on leave from the Department of Political Science at Russell Sage College, Troy, New York. He is the editor of *The Reluctant Pillar: New York and the Adoption of the Federal Constitution* (Albany: New York State Bicentennial Commission, 1988).

HON. SOL WACHTLER, Chief Judge of the State of New York, is chairman of the New York State Bicentennial Commission.

NEW YORK STATE COMMISSION ON THE BICENTENNIAL OF THE UNITED STATES CONSTITUTION

The New York State Bicentennial Commission was established by Chapter 261 of the Laws of 1986, effective July 1, 1986. It is governed by a thirteen-member Commission, chaired by the Honorable Sol Wachtler, Chief Judge of the State of New York.

The purpose of the Commission is "...to promote and coordinate activities to commemorate the bicentennial of the [United States] Constitution and of New York State's role in its ratification."

The Commission began its three-year program in January of 1987. Legislated through December 31, 1989, the Commission has selected annual themes and key events for commemoration. The Commission coordinates and promotes these activities by working with New Yorkers of all ages in all regions of the state. Included in the Commission's agenda are elementary and secondary school programs, public education programs, college and university programs, research and publications, conferences, media programs, and special events.

Cultural Education Center
Room 9D30
Empire State Plaza
Albany, New York 12230